Citizenship in Action

1

SARAH EDWARDS
ANDY GRIFFITH
PETER NORTON
WILL ORD
CLARE RICKETTS

Heinemann

Heinemann Educational Publishers
Halley Court, Jordan Hill, Oxford OX2 8EJ
Part of Harcourt Education

Heinemann is the registered trademark of
Harcourt Education Limited

© Sarah Edwards, Andy Griffith, Peter Norton,
Will Ord, Clare Ricketts, 2003

First published 2003

07 06 05
10 9 8 7 6 5 4 3

British Library Cataloguing in Publication Data is available
from the British Library on request.

10 digit ISBN 0 435 80802 8
13 digit ISBN 978 0 435808 02 0

Edited by Jane Anson
Produced by Wooden Ark

Original illustrations © Harcourt Education Limited, 2003

Illustrated by Joan Corlas, Margaret Jones, The Art Business
Cover design by Jonathan Williams
Printed in China by Everbest
Cover photo: George Clooney © Press Association. Baby orang-
utan, Eye Ubiquitous/ Darren Maybury

Acknowledgements
Every effort has been made to contact copyright holders of material
reproduced in this book. Any omissions will be rectified in
subsequent printings if notice is given to the publishers.

Photo credits:
p.8: A, S&R Greenhill; B, S&R Greenhill; C, Agripicture; D, S&R
Greenhill; E, TRIP; F, Still/Nigel Dickinson; G, Still/Nigel Dickinson;
H, PA Photos/ Michael Walters; I, PA Photos/ Dave Kendall. p.11:
John Walmsley. p.13: A, Popperfoto/Reuters; B, Rex; C, PA Photos.
P.18, Rex Interstock. p.22: A, Rex/Ray Tang; B, Rex/Nils Jorgensen;
C, Shout; D, Rex; E, Rex/Nils. p.23: F, Rex; Group 1: A, The Argus;
B, Rex; C, PA Photos; D, Rex/David Cairns; Group 2: A, Rex; B, PA
Photos/ Malcolm Croft; C, Rex; D, Ronald Grant Archive. p.24: Rex.
P.26: Yiorgis Nikiteas. p.28: PA Photos/ Rui Vieira. p.29: Rex. p.30,
The Argus. p.31: (hydrant and jacket) Photodisc; (danger sign) KPT
Power Photos; (cranes, workers) Corbis. p.32: S&R Greenhill. p.33:
S&R Greenhill. p.34: A, RSPCA/Paul Herrmann; B, Penni Bickle; C,
Photodisc; D, Rex. p.35: E, Photofusion/ Mike McWilliam; F,
RSPCA; G, Still Pictures/ M&C Denis-Huot; H, RSPCA. p.44:
Photodisc. p.45: (fox) Photodisc. p.47: Rex/David Hartley. p.52:
(newsreader) BBC; (Sputnik) Science Photo Library/ David A.
Hardy. p.53: Rex/Nils Jorgensen. p.55: (Coke) Eye Ubiquitous /J
Hazel; (Walkers) Justin Slee. p.57: (Ethiopians) Still/John Isaac; A,
Greenpeace; B, Rex/Geoff Pugh. p.58: PA Photos/ Andrew Parsons.
p.59: A, All Sport/Getty; B, C, D, E, Empics; Sports quiz photos, All
Sport/Getty. p.61: A, Rex/Mark St. George; B, PA Photos/John
Stillwell; C, Rex/Richard Young. p.65: (slaves) Julian Holland
Publishing Ltd; (Greeks) Jeff Edwards & Donald Harley. p.66:
Photodisc. p.67: PA/Matthew Fearn. p.68: (meeting) Taxi;
(footballers) EMPICS. p.69: (children) Still/H Schwarzenbach; (Live
Aid large) Rex; (Live Aid small) Rex/SIPA. p.71: Yiorgos Nikiteas.
p.72: (MP) Rex/Nils Jorgensen; (meeting) PA Photos/ Chris Ison.
p.75: (Blair) Rex; (Queen) Mary Evans Picture Library; (Pope) Rex.
p.77: A, Rex/Tony Kyriacou; B, PA Photos/ Michael Stephens. p.78:
Eye Ubiquitous/A.E. Vizard. p.80-87: Nick Badman. p.88: Vicki Ellis.
p.90-91: Dorton House School. p.92-93: Ivybridge Community
College.

Other credits:
pp.16-17: Extracts from *Lord of the Flies* by William Golding,
reproduced by permission of Faber and Faber Ltd. p.23: ' "Nothing
has changed," says mother of Stephen Lawrence' by Martin Bright,
The Observer 24 February 2002. Reproduced by permission of
Guardian Newspapers Limited. p.25: 'Police Chief says he knows
who killed Lawrence', article from *The Independent*, 28 July 2001,
reproduced by permission of Independent Newspapers (UK)
Limited. p.39: Extracts from the CIWF website reproduced by
permission of CIWF (Compassion in World Farming). p.45: CITES
logo used by permission of CITES (Convention on International
Trade in Endangered Species of Wild Fauna and Flora). p.48:
FilmFour logo used by permission of Channel 4. p.48: Yahoo! UK &
Ireland webpage used by permission of Yahoo! UK Ltd. p.48: Sky
Sports logo reproduced by permission of British Sky Broadcasting
Ltd. p.48: ITV website page used by permission of ITV. p.48: Header
from *Daily Mail* 9 August 2001 used by permission of Atlantic
Syndication. p.48: BBC TV logo reproduced by permission of the
BBC. BBC is a trademark of the British Broadcasting Corporation
and is used under licence. p.52: Front page of *The Independent*, 9
August 2001 reproduced by permission of Independent Newspapers
(UK) Limited. p.52: BBC website reproduced by permission of the
BBC. BBC is a trademark of the British Broadcasting Corporation
and is used under licence. p.53: Article on Greg Dyke from BBC
online reproduced by permission of the BBC, from
http://news.bbc.co.uk/1/hi/uk_politics/379213.stm BBC is a
trademark of the British Broadcasting Corporation and is used
under licence. p.54: 'Refugees are flooding into UK like ants', *Daily
Express* 7 November 2001, reproduced by permission of Express
Newspapers. p.55: Pizza Hut advertisement reproduced by
permission of Freud Communications. p.55: Walkers advertisement
reproduced by permission of Stuart Higgins Communications. p.56:
ASA logo reproduced by permission of ASA (Advertising Standards
Authority) p.57: Pudsey Bear logo reproduced by permission of
BBC Children in Need Appeal.

There are links to relevant web sites in this book. In order to ensure
that the links are up-to-date, that the links work, and that the sites
are not inadvertently linked to sites that could be considered
offensive, we have made the links available on the Heinemann
website at www.heinemann.co.uk/hotlinks. When you access the
site, the express code is 8028P

Tel: 01865 888058   www.heinemann.co.uk

Contents

Introduction

What is Citizenship?

'Citizenship Education is education for citizenship, behaving and acting as a citizen, therefore it is not just knowledge of citizenship and civil society. It also implies developing values, skills and understanding.' (Crick Report, 1998)

Citizenship is a new National Curriculum subject for students at Key Stages 3 and 4. The aim of the Citizenship Programme of Study that you will follow is that you will develop the knowledge and skills you will need in the twenty-first century to become an informed, active and responsible member of a local, national and global community. As well as appreciating your own needs, you will appreciate the needs and views of others.

Some schools may have a timetable period for Citizenship, but most students at Key Stage 3 will develop their Citizenship understanding in a range of different ways. This may include tutor time, PSHE work, as a part of other subjects, within organised events such as the School Council, or in voluntary work in school or the local community.

As a part of your Citizenship programme you will be encouraged to participate and work with others, both at school and in the wider community. At the end of Key Stage 3 you will be assessed by your teachers, who will discuss your progress and involvement in the school's Citizenship programme.

Each of the *Citizenship in Action* student books has been designed to help you understand the key ideas. The books use case studies to help you to understand important Citizenship issues. The text is written to encourage you to react and contribute with your own ideas and thoughts. Each chapter includes key words and definitions. You should try to learn these words and use them in the activities

you will carry out. Many of the activities can be completed alone or with in a group – you could even try them out at home! At the end of each chapter there is a review and reflect section which helps you to pull together the ideas that have been mentioned.

Chapter summaries

Chapter 1 – Citizenship – What's it all about?

This chapter helps you to understand the key ideas behind Citizenship. A school is used as an example of a community. What does it mean to belong to a community? How does a school exercise power and authority, and how are the students encouraged to be involved? This chapter also looks and the rights and responsibilities of young people.

Chapter 2 – Crime and safety awareness

How do you campaign against injustice? With the help of case studies you will become aware of how 'active' citizens have fought injustices. Another case study deals with the important issue of safety at work. The review section asks you to consider how you can bring about change.

Chapter 3 – How does the law protect animals?

The case studies used in this chapter help you to understand how laws are made and changed in the UK. The example of animal welfare will also help you appreciate how different groups can have contrasting views and opinions about these important issues.

Chapter 4 – The media and society

Why does the media have such an impact on our lives? How does it infringe on our privacy? How does the media raise awareness of important world issues and how has it helped make a difference? Why should we be concerned about the power and influence of the media? You will examine and explore some of these ideas in this chapter.

Chapter 5 – How can we make decisions?

In this chapter you will think about who makes decisions on your behalf, and how we choose these people. You will explore ways in which you can get involved in making decisions in your school and community.

Chapter 6 – Developing your school grounds

Using case studies, you will explore different ways of using your school grounds and developing them to benefit everyone. You will consider how important it is for everyone to participate. You will learn the difference between active and passive Citizenship.

Where do you stand now?

As you work through the chapters in the book and the activities you will take part in, think about the following questions:
What are the key Citizenship ideas?
Do you know more about decision-making?
Have you appreciated the views of other people?
Have you take part in discussions and other forms of active Citizenship?

Chapter 1

Citizenship – What's it all about?

Learn about...

Citizenship is about you, the communities you belong to and how you get involved in them. We all have a responsibility towards the people around us, to help make sure they are treated fairly. Of course, other people have responsibilities towards us too. In this unit you will think about:

- How you are involved in the life of your school and local communities.

- How to make it possible for everyone to have their say and listen to the views of others.

- What rights are, and how they relate to responsibilities.

- How our rights and responsibilities change as we get older.

A nuclear family

Playing for a sports team

B

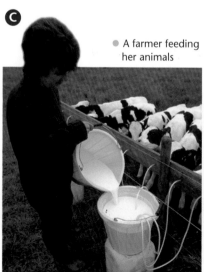
C
A farmer feeding her animals

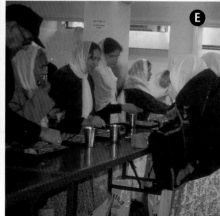
E

D

A dayroom in an old people's home

The langar in a gurdwara

The House of Commons debating chamber

F

Getting technical

Rights things that the law says we can expect from society.

Responsibilities things that we have to do to make sure that rights are used properly.

Citizen an active member of a community.

Community any group of people that you are linked to because you share the same purpose.

John Prescott being 'egged'

I

G

A local protest

H

An 'end Third World debt' protest

Activities

1. Look carefully at the photographs on these two pages. Make a list of some of the different types of community represented.

2. Draw a spider diagram with yourself in the centre. Around the edge write the communities you belong to. Draw lines connecting these communities to the picture of you. Try to think of at least six.

3. Write a paragraph explaining your role in each of your communities. Try to use some of the words from the 'Getting technical' lists.

Extension activity

4. a) In what ways are the people in photograph H showing they are citizens of the world and not just their country?

   b) Who has power in photograph I? Give reasons for your answer.

Belonging to my school

You might never have thought about it like this before, but you are already an active member of a community – your school. After all, where would the teachers be without any pupils to teach? But remember, you're not just there to be taught, you have a role to play in making the school an effective community. A school needs to be a nice place to learn and work. We all (pupils, teachers, support staff, etc.) have a part to play.

Life at primary school

Activities

1 In pairs or groups, talk about your primary schools. Tell each other the following things:

- Did you wear uniform?
- What rules were there?
- What was the playground like?
- What were the teachers like?
- Did you have any special jobs?
- Were you allowed to choose which activities you took part in?
- Were your schools very different?

2 Now you are at secondary school, things will have changed: you have different thoughts and concerns. Draw a picture like the one above, but of your present class. Draw thought bubbles for about ten of the pupils. What might they be thinking about their life at senior school? Here are some ideas to get you started:

- Will I do well in my GCSEs?
- Will I be good enough for the school football team?
- I was scared when the teacher shouted in History.

Activities

3 Think about the good and bad things about being a member of a school community. Record your ideas in a table like the one below. Try to think of examples from your life at primary school and now that you are at secondary school.

Good things about primary school	Bad things about primary school	Good things about secondary school	Bad things about secondary school
Not so many pupils	Not being allowed inside when it's cold at lunchtime	There are some nice teachers	More homework

4 Most schools have a prospectus to show what the school is like. It is usually written by the headteacher and the governors. But it's a long time since they were in Year 7, so imagine they have asked you to write an additional prospectus. Yours should include information and ideas about:

- things to do outside of lessons, e.g. clubs
- how to stay out of trouble
- how to keep school a nice place to work and learn
- what's hot and what's not in the canteen
- people who work in the school (e.g. caretaker, cook, secretaries)
- anything else you think a new pupil should know.

This activity would be ideal for you to use ICT. You could take photographs with a digital camera and word process your text. Maybe you could even create a prospectus on a CD ROM.

Unfortunately, school is not always a good place to be. You made a list of good and bad things about your school. Ideally, the good things outweigh the bad, but for a few people this is not the case.

From the *Metro*, 28 November 2001

Bullied girl kills herself

A girl who saved her dying sister's life has committed suicide after being bullied over her fame.

Elaine Swift, 15, died yesterday after taking an overdose of painkillers. She failed to recover from an emergency liver transplant and contracted septicaemia.

The teenager was hailed a hero when she underwent painful surgery in 1997 to give bone marrow to her sister Christine, then five who had leukaemia.

The transplant was a success but Elaine was bullied when she returned to school because of the publicity she attracted.

Last year, she switched comprehensives in Hartlepool after her parents, Ben and Fiona, became concerned that she was unhappy. However, the taunts continued at her new school, Dyke House.

Mr and Mrs Swift believe Elaine took more than 100 paracetamol tablets after being driven to despair by other pupils. The couple reported Elaine's allegations of bullying to police.

Mr Swift said his daughter had written about taking her own life in a notebook.

He added: 'Elaine thought no-one was taking notice of her bullying claims. The education system failed my daughter. Who will be next?'

Dyke House School insisted it had dealt properly with all the bullying allegations.

A

The School Bully

Times have changed

"Get outta my face!"
"I'll meet you on the school ground after school."
"Watch your back!"
"I saw that look; you can't fool me"

At one time or another, we have all faced acts of intimidation. Whether it was the kid kicking us under our desk, or someone copying our homework, we have all tackled or dodged the school bully. But today's school bullies are more difficult to deal with and we require more strategies to cope with their intensity, lack of fair play and ruthlessness.

Intimidation is the main weapon used by bullies. Physical violence is usually the male form of bullying, while verbal abuse is a more female form of bullying.

Why do bullies bully? According to experts, they are often children from violent backgrounds where children have little or no control over their own environment, and they are often sad, lonely or afraid. They bully to gain a sense of power, to get attention or to feel better about themselves by making someone else feel worse.

How to protect you and your friends from bullying in your school:

- Do not carry weapons, which could be used against you
- Retreat from the bully if possible
- If cornered, talk in a firm, positive manner
- Do not appear timid or scared
- Do not stand and watch others being bullied – go for help from teachers
- Talk to your classmates, and try to promote an environment where bullying is not cool or acceptable
- Promote programmes and discussions about school violence
- Teachers: reward students for dealing with conflict in a non-violent way
- Learn about conflict resolution, peer mediation and anger management techniques
- Help make your school environment a place where its cool to be kind

B

Activities

1. Imagine you were in a situation similar to the person in Extract A. Write diary entries for a week in school, describing:
   - what happened to you
   - how it made you feel
   - what you would like to do about it.

2. Read Extract B. Imagine you plan to start an anti-bullying scheme in your school. Design a poster to recruit other pupils to help you get it started.

Decisions, decisions

A In this country the King could ban anyone from playing football.

B In this country the Prime Minister could not pass a law tomorrow making us all dye our hair pink.

C In this country an adult could not be arrested for carrying a gun.

Getting technical

Power the idea that some people have control or influence over us.

Activities

1 What do you think of a system where the ruler can make any law they like? Try to think of advantages and disadvantages.

2 Are there any rights that a government should never be able to take away from its citizens?

3 Do you think it is a good idea for countries to have some kind of system that prevents the ruler doing just what they want? Explain your answer.

Different countries have different ways of making decisions. In some countries one person can make and change the rules on their own, whereas in other places a democratic process is used to make or change laws. Some countries have a written or traditionally held set of rights that all citizens have. The purpose of a democracy is that all people can somehow have their say in the running of the country. Whatever the situation, decisions cannot be made unless everyone knows what is happening. Without rules about who can make the decisions and how this is done, a country would fall into chaos.

On a smaller scale this is also true at school. If everyone could do what they liked, it would be difficult for anyone to learn. School rules help to safeguard our right to an education, but if the rules were never discussed or changed, we would all still be living in fear of the cane. If your headteacher made all the rules, everyone might have to eat sprouts at lunch, but if the pupils made all the rules, school might start at 10 a.m. and finish at 1 p.m! However, people are more likely to stick to the rules if they have helped to make them in the first place. So how could this happen in practice?

Let's think about the classroom first. Can your citizenship lesson run smoothly if you are all trying to talk at once? Will you learn all you need to if you never sit still? It is important to have rules in the lesson. Think about the rules you are expected to follow in this lesson and why they are important.

Obviously there are some issues that only the headteacher and governors can decide. These could be things like who to employ as teachers and what punishments to use. Sometimes headteachers need to find out what pupils think before a decision can be made. It would be impossible for the headteacher to ask every pupil's opinion, so they might rely on a school council system.

● Sprouts for lunch again!

List of Names for School Council
- Mr Bellamy (Headteacher)
- Miss Alijah (Main Scale Teacher)
- Mrs Knight (Learning Mentor)
- Jatinderpal Singh (Head Boy/Sixth Form rep/Secretary to the council)
- Beverley Peters-Freeman (Head Girl/ Sixth Form rep/Chair of the council)
- Jamie Armstrong (Year 7 rep)
- Susie Finlinson (Year 8 rep)
- Amir Kafai (Year 9 rep)
- Ashok Sharma (Year 10 rep)
- Nazia Ahmed (Year 11 rep)

Enquiry: How can a school council work?

Greenbank School Council Agenda

1. Apologies
2. Agreeing minutes of last meeting
3. 'Wear What You Like Day' – charity initiative
4. Follow up information on improving the school grounds
5. Detentions
6. Year Matters
7. Any Other Business

Greenbank School Council Minutes

Amir Kafai (Year 9 rep) raised the possibility of holding a 'Wear What You Like' day on Friday 17th July to raise money for the local Children's Hospice. He reported that the brother of someone in his year group had recently died of leukaemia and the family had received a lot of support from the hospice. This boy was keen to give something back to the hospice and he felt that it would be nice to raise some money for them and was hoping that the school would support him in this.

Mr Bellamy (Headteacher) commented that whilst he was keen to help this boy raise money for the hospice, he was concerned about the impact a non-uniform day would have on pupils. He said that behaviour was inclined to deteriorate when pupils were out of uniform and that some pupils did not like coming to school wearing their own clothes for fear of what others would think of them.

Mrs Knight (Learning Mentor) mentioned that this was the last day of term and debate followed about whether it was a good idea to do something different on this day or if it would be more sensible to hold it earlier in the term.

It was suggested (by Jatinderpal Singh) that it would be more sensible to hold the event the week before (10th July) so that poor behaviour could be punished.

The council voted on the issue and they unanimously agreed that the event should take place on 10th July.

ACTION: Amir Kafai to arrange for a person from the hospice to come and speak at the whole school assembly to promote the cause.

Mr Bellamy to produce a letter to be sent home to parents informing them of the event.

> I'm really pleased. I wanted to do something for the Hospice that helped my family and the school council has helped me to do that.

Look at the pictures on the left and at the bottom of page 14, showing how a school council works. Discuss the questions in pairs.

- What was the problem raised?
- How did the council deal with the issue?
- How successful was the council?

Activities

Imagine you are a member of your school council.

1. Write a list of people who would attend the meetings.

2. What things might have to be done before each meeting? (E.g. ask your tutor group what issues should be raised.)

3. Write the agenda for a meeting (remember to include the issue raised below).

4. Your form has asked you to raise the issue of putting a chocolate machine in the canteen. The headteacher needs to be persuaded that this is a good idea. Write down the argument you will use to do this.

5. Imagine that somebody else argued against this issue. Write down the argument they might have used.

6. Write the section of the minutes that records the decision that was made.

7. Do you think a school council is a good idea? Give reasons for your answer.

Help!

An **agenda** is a list of the things that will be discussed at a meeting. The first item on the agenda is usually to read the minutes of the last meeting and agree that they are correct. In the middle you will have all the issues to be raised. The last item is usually 'Any Other Business', which is an opportunity for people to raise other issues that are not already on the agenda.

The **minutes** of the meeting are an account of what took place in the meeting. The decisions that were taken are recorded and some of the main points of discussion are noted down.

Survivor!

We're on an island. We've been on the mountain-top and seen water all around. We saw no houses, no smoke, no footprints, no boats, no people. We're on an uninhabited island with no other people on it … There aren't any grown-ups. We shall have to look after ourselves.

The quotation on the left is taken from *Lord of the Flies*, a book about a group of boys who find themselves stranded on a desert island. There are no adults on the island and the boys are not sure if anyone knows where they are, so they realise that they will need to make some big decisions if they are to survive.

A

'Seems to me we ought to have a chief to decide things.'
'A chief! A chief!'
'I ought to be chief,' said Jack with simple arrogance, 'because I'm chapter chorister and head boy. I can sing C sharp.'
Another buzz.
'Well then,' said Jack, 'I–'
He hesitated. The dark boy, Roger, stirred at last and spoke up.
'Let's have a vote.'
'Yes!'
'Vote for a chief!'
'Let's vote–'

Q *What qualities do you think a leader should have? Why?*

B

(Ralph) 'And another thing. We can't have everybody talking at once. We'll have to have "Hands up" like at school'…
Jack was on his feet.
'We'll have rules!' he cried excitedly. 'Lots of rules! Then when anyone breaks 'em–'

C

(Ralph) 'There was a ship. Out there. You said you'd keep the fire going and you let it out!' …
(Piggy) 'You and your blood, Jack Merridew! You and your hunting! We might have gone home–' …
(Jack) 'The job was too much. We needed everyone.'

Q *What do you think should happen to a person who breaks rules? Does it make any difference what the rule is or who made it?*

Q *How do you think the jobs should be shared out in a desert island scenario? Is there any job that everyone should do?*

First they choose a leader – Ralph (Extract A). He looks after the conch (a special shell which can be blown through to make a noise). The conch is used to call all the boys to meetings where decisions will be made (Extract B).

Things they need to think about:
• how to keep warm
• what to eat
• what to do about sanitation
• how to increase their chance of being rescued.

Decisions they make:
• to build shelters
• to eat fruit from trees and hunt pigs for meat
• to use a certain place only for a toilet
• to build a fire so passing ships can find them.

As time goes on, things go wrong. Jack becomes so obsessed with hunting that he neglects the fire and it goes out, just before a ship passes (Extract C). In the end, everything gets so bad that two of the boys – Simon and Piggy – are killed. Jack becomes power-crazed (Extract D) and turns most of the others against Ralph. When rescue finally arrives, the group has fallen apart (Extract E) and there is no community left.

D (Jack) 'Who'll join my tribe?'
  'I will.'
  'Me.'
  'I will.'
  'I'll blow the conch,' said Ralph breathlessly, 'and call an assembly.'
  'We shan't hear it.'

Q *What sort of things can happen when people want too much power for themselves and don't think about their responsibilities towards others?*

E (The naval officer) 'Who's boss here?'
  'I am,' said Ralph loudly …
  'We saw your smoke. And you don't know how many of you there are?'
  'No, sir.'
  'I should have thought,' said the officer as he visualised the search before him, 'I should have thought that a pack of British boys–you're all British aren't you?–would have been able to put up a better show than that–I mean–'
  'It was like that at first,' said Ralph, 'before things–'
  He stopped.
  'We were together then– '

Q *What do you think went wrong? You could read* Lord of the Flies *yourself to find out more.*

Extension activity

1 How do you think a community is affected by its size?

2 Can you think of a situation when rights and responsibilities might clash?

3 If someone fails to carry out their responsibilities, should they lose some of their rights?

4 When is it acceptable to take away someone's rights? When is it unacceptable?

How things change

Babies need to have most things done for them and they can't do much for other people. As we get older we can do more for ourselves, but it is also reasonable for people to expect that we can do things for them. This is how rights and responsibilities balance out.

What rights does this baby have?

Who is responsible for naming this baby?

List three things this baby might need protecting from.

Who will protect the baby's rights?

List three hopes that the parents of this baby might have for it as it is growing up.

List three things it can't do for itself.

Who might do these things for the child?

Does this baby have any responsibilities?

19

18
17
16
15
14
13
12
11
10
9
8
7
6
5
4
3
2

Birth

Activities

1 Choose three of the questions above and write your answers to them.

2 On a timeline like the one on the left, complete the following tasks in different coloured pens:

a) Mark in one colour the age at which the law allows you to:
- buy alcohol
- have sex
- drive a car
- vote
- work
- buy a pet
- buy cigarettes
- buy lottery tickets
- get married.

b) Mark in another colour the age at which you are allowed to:
- travel to school on your own
- stay over at your friend's house
- have your own door key
- choose your own clothes
- go into town on your own.

c) Mark in a third colour the age at which you think you should:
- make your own bed
- help look after your younger brothers or sisters
- help with the housework
- cook dinner for your family
- open a bank account.

3 Each of the people opposite is talking about a right, a responsibility and a skill. In a table like the one below, record the right, the responsibility and the skill that each one is talking about. The first one has been done for you.

Person	Right	Responsibility	Skill
(factory worker)	Safe working conditions	Checking quality of components	Being a good listener

As you get older you will take on more roles in your community. This will give you a chance to use skills you've already got and to develop new ones. You will also get more rights, but with these will come increased responsibilities.

A

I'm in charge of quality control in my factory. I have to make sure that all the components we make are the right size. My employers have to make sure the factory is a safe place to work. People come and tell me their problems, so they elected me union rep.

B

Look what Jayne painted for me today! I pick Jayne up from school because her Mum works. I really enjoy the time we spend together each day. I'm lucky, some of my friends don't get to see their grandchildren so often.

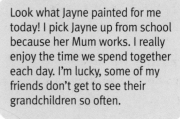

C

We've had a few problems in our flats recently with vandalism. Some of the older people were scared, so a group of us decided to take action. After a lot of hard work and with a council grant we've set up a youth club for the kids and a befriending scheme for the old people. Everyone's happier now.

I love shopping! I've got a really good eye for a bargain. I once had to take something back to a shop because it was faulty. They gave me my money back. I try and make sure that I buy things that are fairly traded – that means the people who made the goods get paid a fair price for their work.

D

E

This is my first time voting – I'm only just 18. It might not seem like much, but I know there are some countries where people don't get the opportunity to vote. I spent some time reading about each of the candidates and I voted for the one I most agreed with.

F

It's great to be back at work. I've just been in hospital having my appendix removed. The staff at the hospital were great. I pay quite a lot of tax because my business is successful, but I don't mind because the government needs that money for schools and lots of other things as well as hospitals.

We're going to France in the summer. I thought it would be a good thing if I knew what to say when I got there. I didn't find learning very easy when I was at school, but I'm really enjoying this. I've just discovered that there are free courses for people who are out of work, so I'm going to tell my friend Bruce, who's just lost his job.

G

Review and reflect

In this unit you have learned about what it means to be an active citizen with rights and responsibilities. You have thought about rules and democratic decision-making at school and in other communities. You have considered how personal rights and responsibilities change with age, and how they interact with other people's rights and responsibilities. You have had the opportunity to work on your own and with others to improve your understanding of how an effective community works. Hopefully now you are enthusiastic about putting what you've learned into action!

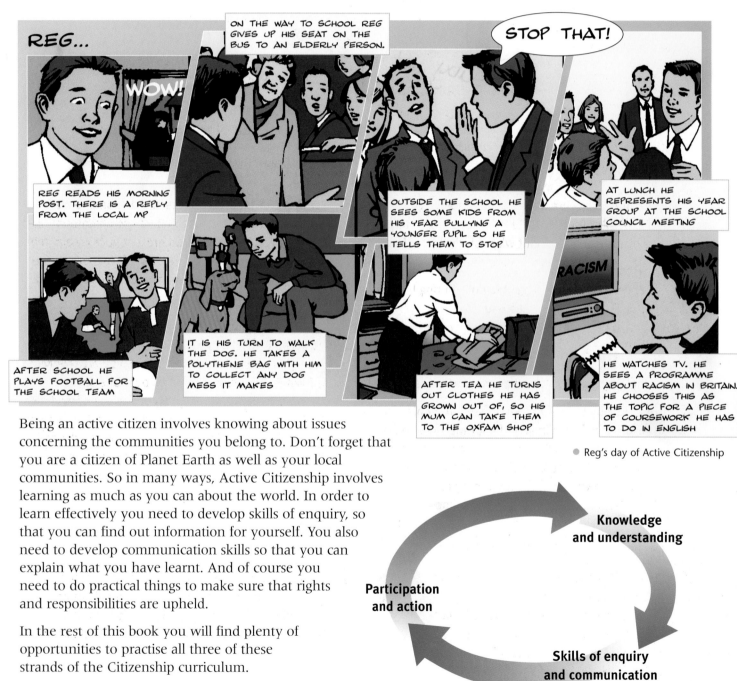

Reg's day of Active Citizenship

Being an active citizen involves knowing about issues concerning the communities you belong to. Don't forget that you are a citizen of Planet Earth as well as your local communities. So in many ways, Active Citizenship involves learning as much as you can about the world. In order to learn effectively you need to develop skills of enquiry, so that you can find out information for yourself. You also need to develop communication skills so that you can explain what you have learnt. And of course you need to do practical things to make sure that rights and responsibilities are upheld.

In the rest of this book you will find plenty of opportunities to practise all three of these strands of the Citizenship curriculum.

Knowledge and understanding

Skills of enquiry and communication

Participation and action

Activities

1 Complete a spider diagram like the one below to summarise what you have learnt in this chapter. Try to do it without copying directly from the Getting technical boxes.

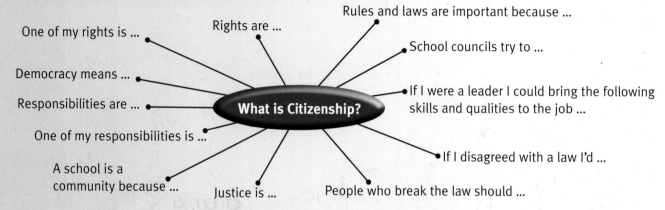

Compare your sentences with somebody else's in the class. Are there any places where you totally disagree? If so, talk about why you disagree. Does it matter? Can you resolve your differences?

2 a) Make a list of the things Reg does during his day of Active Citizenship (see page 20).
   b) List some of the different communities involved in Reg's day.
   c) List some of the rights, responsibilities and skills that Reg actively demonstrates during the day.

3 Are there any things that Reg does during his day that you cannot use in any of your answers above? This is probably because you do not understand or know about the issues or situations concerned. Where could you try to find out more about them? Write a list of ways you would try to find out more.

4 Choose one of Reg's actions and do some research about the rights, responsibilities and community that are involved in it. You could present your research as a display using literature you have found or created yourself, or you could give a verbal presentation to the rest of your class.

5 Now think about your own Active Citizenship. What do you do already to help promote rights and responsibilities in the communities you are involved in? What new things could you do? Take some practical action now and produce a piece of evidence that testifies to what you have done. Start your own Citizenship portfolio now and keep your evidence in it. Don't forget to add more evidence each time you have some.

Extension activity

6 Create an information point at school where pupils can post details of opportunities to get involved in Active Citizenship. This could also include reports of things that pupils have already done. You will need to make sure that the information point is maintained and kept up to date.

7 If your school has a website, you could include details of Citizenship activities that pupils have been involved in. You might like to look at this example: go to www.heinemann.co.uk/hotlinks and click on this activity.

Chapter 2

Crime and safety awareness

Learn about...

- Why justice is important.
- Why people start a campaign and the methods that they use.
- How miscarriages of justice have happened.
- How people don't always know about their right to a safe working environment.
- How campaigns have changed the law.

● The Potters Bar rail crash

● Child protesting

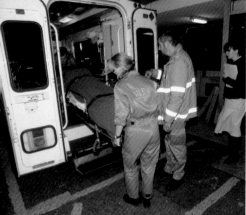

● After an accident at work ...

● The Birmingham six after release from prison

● Stephen Lawrence memorial plaque

Getting technical

Justice the way laws and rules are used to ensure fair treatment within a community.

'Nothing has changed', says mother of Stephen Lawrence

The mother of Stephen Lawrence, who was stabbed to death in London in April 1993, told a conference that nothing had changed since the government pledged to root out prejudice three years ago. Doreen Lawrence told an audience of 200 that she had received racist hate mail.

She was accompanied by a police protection officer at the conference, organised by the National Assembly Against Racism to mark the third anniversary of the Macpherson report on the failed police investigation into her son's death.

She said: 'We as black people are still on the outside looking in. That has not changed since the report came out. I am bringing somebody here to protect my safety because of the racist hate mail that is being sent to this conference.'

In a separate report from the Institute of Race Relations (IRR) they estimate that there have been over fifty racially motivated murders since the death of Stephen Lawrence and hundreds of racially motivated attacks.

● From the *Observer*, 24 February 2002

Activities

1 Discussion questions

- What does Mrs Lawrence mean by saying she had received racist hate mail?
- Why does she say that 'nothing has changed' since her son's death?
- What does 'justice' mean?
- Why is justice so important to Doreen Lawrence?
- Why are justice and fairness important?
- Are there rules, laws or situations in your life that seem to be unjust or unfair? What are they?

2 Group 1

Simon Jones

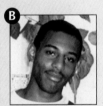
Stephen Lawrence

Carl Bridgewater

Ronnie Biggs

3 Group 2

Judith Ward

Stefan Kiszko

Stephen Downing

Andy Dufresne
(from the film
Shawshank Redemption)

Your teacher will give you some information about these people.

- What do/did these people have in common?
- Which one is the 'odd one out' in each of the two groups?
- Think about what your teacher has told you, and write down two things that surprised you and two things that you didn't know.
- Compare your notes with a partner's. Are your ideas similar?
- What do you think about the fairness of these cases?
- As a citizen, what can you do to change things that seem to be unfair?

Case Study 1: The murder of Stephen Lawrence

● Stephen Lawrence

Stephen Lawrence was 18 years old; he was studying for his A-Levels in Eltham, London. On 22 April 1993 he was murdered while waiting for a bus with a friend. His murderers have never been caught.

At 10.30 p.m. a group of five or six white youths surrounded Stephen. He was stabbed. He died from 12cm deep stab wounds in his chest.

Stephen's friend, Duwayne Brooks, desperately tried to stop cars so that someone would help, but no one would stop. When a couple stopped to help, Duwayne went to call an ambulance.

Police officers arrived, but no one tried to stop Stephen's bleeding. The police knew which way the gang had run after the attack, but they did not carry out a house-to-house search because they felt it was too late to disturb people.

Over the next few days, the police received several tip-offs. All of them named the same members of a local white gang who carried knives. But the police did not arrest anyone until two weeks later. The delay gave the attackers time to clean up evidence that might link them with the murder, such as weapons, or blood on their clothing.

When the police searched the suspects' homes, they found knives but no traces of any blood. The charges against the gang – David Norris, Jamie Acourt, Neil Acourt, Gary Dobson and Luke Knight – had to be dropped because there was not enough evidence against them.

Mr and Mrs Lawrence felt that the police were insensitive towards them right from the start. The police refused to accept that the attack was based on racism. They suggested that Stephen must have provoked the gang. The Police Inspector at the hospital where Stephen was taken had said to them, 'We've got a young lad in there. He's dead … If it's not your son, then all well and good, but we need to know.'

The Lawrence family began to campaign for justice. They began a private prosecution against the five suspects. Amongst the evidence was a video taken secretly in 1994. It showed the suspects holding knives and pretending to kill black people. The gang were acquitted due to lack of evidence.

The campaign was granted an inquest into Stephen's death. The five suspects were called to the inquest. They refused to answer questions and left in an arrogant manner. This led the *Daily Mail* to print a front page with photographs of the suspects under the headline 'MURDERERS'. The suspects decided not to sue the newspaper for libel.

The government set up a public inquiry into Stephen's murder and the police investigation. The inquiry's report criticised the police, especially for not being sensitive towards Duwayne Brooks and Stephen's family, and for taking too long to gather evidence.

The report also criticised the police for stereotyping black people. This supported Duwayne Brooks, who said, 'The police treated me like a liar, like a suspect instead of a victim, because I was black and they couldn't believe that white boys would attack us for nothing. They tried at the police station to get me to say that the attackers didn't call us nigger. They described me as violent, uncooperative, intimidating. They were stereotyping me as a young black male.'

The report concluded that the police might have acted differently if Stephen had been white. It said that racism includes 'attitudes and behaviour that amount to discrimination through unwitting prejudice, ignorance, thoughtlessness and racist stereotyping.' Where these attitudes are found in an organisation such as the police, that organisation is said to suffer from 'institutional racism'. The Prime Minister has promised that the Government will oppose racism in all organisations, including the police, schools and hospitals.

The Independent (July 2001)

THE INDEPENDENT

Police chief says he knows who killed Lawrence

By Jason Bennetto
28 July 2001

The head of the Metropolitan Police insisted yesterday that he knew who killed the black student Stephen Lawrence and said he still hoped to bring the murderers to justice.

Sir John Stevens, the Commissioner of the Met, said his officers were still working hard to find new evidence, including scientific material, with which to prosecute the suspects.

The 18-year-old was stabbed to death by a gang of white racists at a bus stop in Eltham, south-east London in April 1993.

Five suspects, Neil and Jamie Acourt, Luke Knight, Gary Dobson and David Norris were arrested by police and charged with Stephen's murder.

Neil Acourt, Gary Dobson and Luke Knight were formally acquitted when a private prosecution for murder failed and cases against the other suspects were dropped.

During a telephone phone-in with Sir John on BBC Radio Five Live the police chief was asked if he knew who killed Stephen. He replied: "Yes."

He added: "We will proceed with investigations and see what we can do with that. We certainly haven't given up on the investigation."

He agreed that most people who had read reports about the case in the media would be aware who was the focus of the investigations.

Later when challenged about the prospects of a successful conviction he replied that there are now many cases coming before juries which due to advances in forensics and other techniques could not have been considered in previous years.

"We'll never give up while we think we have evidence that will take people before the courts.

"We're still on the case and will still be on the case while there's hope that we can convict these people," he said.

During yesterday's radio programme, Duwayne Brooks, the 18-year-old friend of Stephen who witnessed the stabbing, asked the Commissioner why police were still investigating the killing.

Mr Brooks, who is suing the Metropolitan Police for negligence over his treatment, said it was a "waste of taxpayers' money" because no one would ever be charged. Sir John replied: "John Grieve, who is heading up the investigation, would not pursue these avenues of inquiry unless he thought they were going to get a result. "We owe it to you and to the Lawrence family."

Mr Brooks said: "We know it's impossible for these guys to face trial."

The Government is considering whether to scrap Double Jeopardy – the rule that prevents defendants being tried twice for the same crime – in serious cases such as murder.

In July 2001, the head of the Metropolitan Police in London, Sir John Stevens, stated that he knew the name of Stephen's killer. But because of the 'Double Jeopardy' rule it is not possible to try someone for the same crime twice. This means that if someone has been found innocent of a crime, they cannot be charged and taken to court again.

Activities

1 **Talking/thinking points – group work**
Duwayne Brooks said that the police 'stereotyped' him and Stephen. What does this mean?

Some people use statements that begin with the word 'all', such as 'all white people are greedy'. The words 'all' and 'some' are important. Make up ten sentences about people, beginning with the word 'all'. Discuss your sentences, then decide whether you should replace some of the 'alls' with the word 'some'. Feedback your ideas with other groups.

- The head of the Metropolitan Police says he knows who killed Stephen. What do you feel about this?
- How would you feel if your son had been murdered but the killers had never been prosecuted?
- What could be done to make Stephen's family and friends feel that justice had been done?
- Some people would argue that a lot has been done to tackle institutional racism. Conduct a survey and/or contact your local police community liaison officer to find out what they have done to change.

Extension activity

1 Use the Internet, books and newspapers to find out more about Stephen.

2 In the USA there is a national holiday on the birthday of civil-rights leader Martin Luther King. What if we had a Stephen Lawrence Memorial Day in Britain?

3 Devise events for your school. You can call the day anything you wish: 'Justice Day' or 'Stephen Lawrence Day' are just two ideas.

4 What budget would you receive from the school? Could you raise more to boost this?

5 Decide what facilities you would need, e.g. hall, classroom space, TV and video, etc.

6 Who would you invite? E.g. speakers, musicians, artists, etc.

7 What films, music, artwork, stories, poems could be used for display and discussion? Liaise with subject teachers and undertake other research on 'justice' and 'racism'.

● Children planning a campaign

The Double Jeopardy rule

In English law it is not possible to try someone twice for the same crime. This law dates back to Roman times. It has been part of English common law since the 12th century.

The youths who were acquitted of the murder of Stephen Lawrence when they were privately prosecuted, cannot be tried again, even if there is new evidence against them.

Some lawyers think the Double Jeopardy rule should be abolished in murder cases where there is 'compelling' new evidence. In such cases a second trial should be allowed. Others, however, think that the rule should stay.

Arguments for keeping the Double Jeopardy rule
Second trials would be unfair because juries would be sure to convict if they knew that a re-trial was based on evidence that the appeal court had found 'compelling'.

If the police were allowed two chances to gather evidence and convict people they might be less thorough.

Arguments for abandoning the Double Jeopardy rule
There have been many cases where people have been cleared of murders they actually did commit. There is nothing to stop them bragging about what they have done and how they got away with it.

Plenty of re-trials happen already, for example where the jury cannot agree on a verdict, or when a member of the jury dies.

Activities

1. Prepare a debate on the Double Jeopardy rule. Prepare arguments for and against.

2. Use ICT to present your findings, with graphs to show the percentage of people who support each argument.

3. What are your personal opinions on this rule?

4. Gather opinions from other people in your school to support your argument.

Case study 2: The Stephen Downing case

● Stephen Downing (aged 17)

In September 1973, a 32-year-old secretary called Wendy Sewell was clubbed to death in Bakewell cemetery, Derbyshire. Her body was found by a 17-year-old who had learning difficulties. His name was Stephen Downing, and he worked as a gardener in the cemetery. After many hours of police questioning, Stephen confessed to killing Wendy. As it turned out, he was innocent.

At his trial, Stephen retracted his confession and pleaded not guilty. Nevertheless, he was found guilty and sentenced to 17 years in prison. Stephen could have walked free in 1991, but he continued to protest his innocence. He was therefore classified as an IDOM – a prisoner in denial of murder – which meant that he could not be released.

During his time in prison, Stephen was stabbed, scalded with hot water and beaten up. His parents started a campaign to get his case reviewed. They were supported by Don Hale, the editor of a local newspaper. His investigation revealed new witnesses and information that had not been available at Stephen's trial.

One witness had seen Wendy embracing a man at the cemetery who was definitely not Stephen.

Another witness saw Stephen leaving the cemetery for his lunch break, before Wendy arrived. A third witness described a blood-stained man – not Stephen – running out of the cemetery 'like a bat out of hell'.

The police had dismissed some of these witnesses because they were convinced Stephen was guilty. Other witnesses had been afraid to come forward. One wrote anonymously to Don Hale, telling how she had been with a lover in the woods on the day of the murder and had heard shouting. She had seen a man running away and then Stephen arriving at the graveyard, and bending over Wendy's body.

It seemed that a number of people in Bakewell knew who the real murderer was. Don Hale received death threats and was nearly killed by two hit-and-run drivers. Clearly, somebody did not want him to discover the truth.

When Stephen was arrested he was not allowed to have a solicitor. He was questioned on his own for nine hours, and eventually, tired and hungry, he signed a confession saying that he had struck Wendy twice around the back of the head and killed her.

When the forensic evidence was examined again, DNA results proved that a palm-print on Wendy's body and fibres on the murder weapon were not Stephen's and that she must have been hit up to eight times in the attack.

In 1997, 3,500 Bakewell residents signed a petition calling for Stephen's release. In 2001, he was released and returned home. He had spent over 27 years in prison for a crime he did not commit.

Stephen Downing after his release from prison

Activities

1. Stephen Downing was a victim of a 'miscarriage of justice'. Explain what this means.

2. There have been many changes in the way police interview suspects. Which of the statements below are TRUE and which are FALSE?
   - Police have to tape-record interviews with suspects.
   - There must be at least two eyewitnesses to a crime to get a conviction.
   - Suspects have the right to a ten-minute beak every hour during interrogation.
   - Suspects have the right to have a solicitor present when they are being questioned by police at a police station.

3. Look again at your answers to question 2. What would you add to these to help people with learning difficulties understand what is happening to them?

4. Don Hale is obviously a determined man. What other qualities are needed to run a campaign that could go on for years?

5. Produce a piece of work that highlights the injustice of Stephen Downing's story. You might:
   - Write a story/poem either about Stephen Downing or imagining you are him.
   - Draw a picture/poster calling for justice for Stephen Downing.
   - Write a song/rap.
   - Design and make a board game on injustice.

6. Dramatise events in Stephen's life, e.g. his first night in prison or the day he was released.

7. Over 3,500 people signed a petition for Stephen's release. Have any issues in your community or school led to someone to start a petition? If you were organising a petition, who would you present it to?

8. Stephen would have been released earlier if he had pleaded guilty, even though he was innocent. He was not released because he was a prisoner IDOM (in denial of murder). Explain why he did this. What would you have done in his position?

Case study 3: The Simon Jones Campaign

● Simon Jones

While taking a year out from university, 24-year-old Simon Jones was taken on as a casual worker at Shoreham docks. On 24 April 1998, within hours of starting work, his head was almost severed by the grab of a crane. Simon had been unloading cargo inside a ship. This is a dangerous job, but he had received only a few minutes' 'training'.

The number of casual workers, or 'casuals', is growing. They are doing low-paid jobs with no guarantee how long the job will last, no sick pay, no holiday pay and little training. At the same time that this growth in the employment of casuals has occurred, the number of deaths at work has been increasing. Internationally, 1.3 million people are killed every year through accidents and work-related illnesses – that's more than 3,300 deaths per day. In the UK alone, up to 3,000 workers die every year from asbestos-related disease.

Simon Jones's family and friends started The Simon Jones Memorial Campaign to end the use of casual workers and to improve Health and Safety in the workplace. Each year the Health and Safety Executive is able to investigate only about 5% of serious injuries at work (like being blinded or losing a limb) because they do not have enough inspectors.

Even when deaths are investigated and a company is proven to be at fault, the penalties against employers can be extremely light. In November 1999, Frank O'Toole was killed when pallets of cardboard fell off a lorry on to his motorbike. Express Corrugated Cases Ltd of High Wycombe broke a number of health and safety laws. They were fined £10,000.

In December 2001, Brian Knight fell from the roof of the Imperial War Museum while working. An inquest declared that his death was 'unlawful', but no one has been prosecuted.

● Number of deaths/injuries at work in the last few years in the UK

Workplace deaths	
1999/00	220 deaths
2000/01	295 deaths

The Simon Jones Memorial Campaign want to see a law that holds one of the directors of a large company personally responsible for Health and Safety in their organisation. This person would be liable to prosecution if their company was found to have ignored Health and Safety laws. Many campaigners on improving workers' safety think that this will help reduce deaths at work, as company directors will risk going to prison if a worker in their company dies needlessly. Most deaths at work are avoidable. The more information and training that workers and the public get about safety, the fewer deaths and injuries there will be.

Activities

1. The Trades Union Congress (TUC) also campaigns for workers' safety. Cases and campaign information can be found at their website. Go to www.heinemann.co.uk/hotlinks and click on this activity. Examine some cases where there have been successful prosecutions. Record the details of each case and the level of the fine. Many of the fines are small, even in cases where people have died. What do you think about these fines?

2. The Simon Jones Memorial Campaign has used a variety of methods to raise awareness of the issues around the increase in casual workers. They have used direct action such as 'sit-ins' and 'occupations' of offices and the docks where Simon died. These actions are illegal as the campaigners could be arrested for trespass. Discuss whether breaking one law to change another is responsible behaviour.

3. In your group, research other campaigns that have used non-violent, direct-action methods. The Women's Suffrage Movement is one example (you could ask your History teacher about this).

4. Contact the Health and Safety Executive, the organisation responsible for investigating and prosecuting companies that have broken safety laws. Go to www.heinemann.co.uk/hotlinks and click on this activity.

Review and reflect

School campaign: Active Citizens

Over the last few years there has been concern that a lot of things in our society are not going too well. Crime figures are high, fewer people are voting and fewer people seem to be getting involved in the life of their communities. There has been a call for schools to do something about this and not just leave it to parents. Some people say that schools should just teach the 'three Rs' – Reading, wRiting and aRithmetic. Others say that two more Rs should be added – to teach the difference between Right and wRong.

● School pupils at breaktime

Activities

1. How does your school demonstrate the difference between right and wrong?

2. Over the last few years, School Councils have grown in Britain. Why do you think this is?

3. Who is involved in your School Council? What have they done to improve your school?

4. What issues should your School Council take up?

5. What could your School Council do to make people more aware of personal safety issues such as mobile phone thefts and walking home from school?

● Girl using a mobile phone

Extension activity

6. Use local newspapers, national newspapers, the Internet, etc. to build a scrapbook or collage of any current campaigns.

7. Choose one of these and do a presentation on it to the rest of the class. The campaign should preferably be one that you support (if not, you will have to pretend to support it for this activity).

   Use your presentation to persuade others to support the campaign. Your teacher will give you some advice on how to deliver a presentation.

8. Prepare a presentation of how the legal system works. Show what roles different people and courts play in the system.

Chapter 3

How does the law protect animals?

Learn about...

As you will already know, in this country we have laws which help society to function. In this unit you will learn more about how these laws are made and enforced. You will discover that laws can be made at local, national and international levels. You will also look at the role played by individuals and groups in influencing legislation at each of these levels. In this unit we will look at these issues by considering how the law protects animals. But what you learn in this unit is also relevant to laws about other aspects of our lives. In the following pages you will be exploring these questions:

- How does the law protect our pets?
- How does the law protect animal welfare?
- How does parliament debate an issue?
- How is animal welfare of concern internationally?

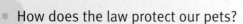

E

F

Getting technical

Legislation the process of making laws; also the collective term for laws.

Influence an attempt by individuals or groups to persuade parliament to take account of their opinions.

G

H

Activities

1 In pairs, discuss the pictures on these pages. Think about how they make you feel and why. Choose the three pictures that you feel most strongly about. For each one, write a description of what you can see and explain your feelings about it.

2 Are there any questions you would like to ask about the pictures to help you understand them better? Choose one of the pictures and write a list of the questions you would like to ask about it.

3 The pictures have been chosen to illustrate some of the terms from the 'Getting technical' lists throughout the chapter. Can you see how? Remember that there might be more than one link to each word or picture. Complete a table like the one below to show some of the links. The first one has been done for you. (You can use pictures more than once.)

Word	Example from the pictures
Legislation	Picture C shows a person with their pet. By law you cannot own a pet until you are 12 years old.

How does the law protect our pets?

The British are renowned for being a nation of animal lovers. According to the RSPCA, 60% of UK households have a pet.

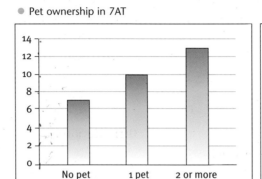

● Pet ownership in 7AT

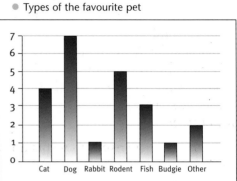

● Types of the favourite pet

Activities

The bar charts above show how many pupils in a class have pets at home, and what those pets are.

1 Collect data on how many people in your class do not have a pet at home, how many have just one and how many have two or more. Draw a bar chart to display your results.

2 Collect data on the animals owned by people in your class. Use the same headings as the 'Types of pet' chart above. If people have more than one pet, they must choose their favourite pet for the data. Display these results in a second bar chart.

So, why do people have pets? Reasons could include the need for companionship, a desire to care for something, or even to help them to relax. Can you think of any others?

People over 12 have the right to own a pet, but remember that rights come with responsibilities.

> I'd like a dog but a big one would need lots of walks

> I'd like some chickens but would they wake the neighbours?

> I'd like a rabbit but I'd have to build a secure hutch so the foxes wouldn't get it

> I'd like a snake but I'm not sure what specialist equipment they'd need

> I'd like a horse but could I afford the vet's bills and stabling fees?

> I'd like a cat but I'd need to get it neutered to avoid unwanted kittens

> I'd like a pot-bellied pig but have I got room in the garden?

Activities

1 Make a drawing like the one above. Fill in the thought bubbles with 'I'd like a … but …' Your ideas should be different from the ones on this page.

Is keeping a pet a personal matter?

We have seen that keeping a pet involves lots of responsibilities. It can be difficult to care for a pet properly and sometimes things go wrong. Some people deliberately mistreat animals, others do it by mistake because of ignorance. They may not know what a particular animal needs, or they may even have chosen an animal that is not suitable as a pet for anyone.

So how can we ensure that this does not happen? In this country the law steps in to regulate matters.

Do you think the law should be involved in the issue of pet ownership? How do you think the law is involved?

Here are some examples of what the law says:

- *Dangerous Dogs Act 1991* restricts how you keep certain breeds of dog.
- *Protection of Animals Act 1911* says you cannot cause unnecessary suffering to animals.
- *Performing Animals (Regulation) Act 1925* says that anyone who keeps or trains animals for public performance needs a licence.

These laws are very well meaning but if no one puts them into practice then they are a waste of time. So it's very important to make sure that the laws are enforced. One way to do this is through the work of charities such as the RSPCA who can, for example, remove a pet from an owner who has mistreated it. The RSPCA runs centres to care for such animals until they can be re-homed with responsible owners. RSPCA officers also sometimes prepare the case notes which are used to prosecute people who have mistreated animals.

Another way that the government ensures a law is effective is to give local authorities special powers of enforcement. These are called by-laws, particularly if local knowledge is needed. For example in Birmingham:

"The Environmental and Consumer Services Department has a statutory responsibility to enforce animal health and welfare regulations concerning the keeping, movement and sale of both pet and commercially traded animals, including livestock. Premises including pet shops, boarding kennels, catteries, circuses and zoos are inspected as well as vehicles transporting live animals."

Getting technical

Charity this is similar to a pressure group, but it is funded through donations.

Activities

1. How would you punish someone who has mistreated an animal? Write a paragraph to explain your answer. Show that you have thought about the following things:

    - Does it make a difference how badly the animal was treated?
    - What if the animal died?
    - Does it make a difference if the mistreatment was done through ignorance rather than deliberately?
    - Does it depend who has mistreated the animal?

    ICT Research your local authority's website. Look for examples of how laws made by the government are enforced by your authority at a local level.

How does the law safeguard animal welfare?

Have you ever thought about all the different ways human beings use animals?

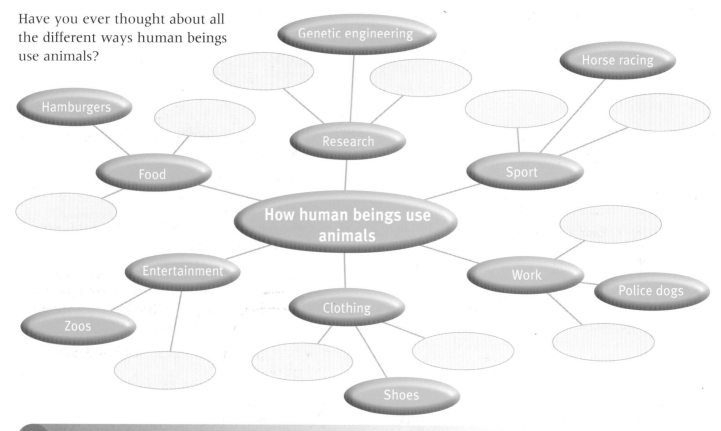

Activities

1. On a chart like the one above, write down all the ways you can think of that animals are used for food, research, sport, work, clothing and entertainment.

2. Can you think of any other areas where human beings use animals? Add them to your chart.

3. Put a circle around any of the things that you think are cruel to animals.

4. In a different colour, circle any things that you think the law regulates.

Sometimes the law allows people to treat animals in a way that might be considered cruel, for example factory farming and medical testing. This is because Parliament has decided, often after a lot of debate, that some animal suffering can be justified if human beings benefit from it. The law tries to draw a line beyond which the suffering would be unacceptable.

When laws like this are being made, Parliament is influenced by lots of different people. Individuals have the right to make their feelings known but they often feel that it is more effective to work with other people. An organised group that may try to lobby Parliament is called a pressure group. There can also be problems when a law has been passed, because not everyone will agree that the line has been drawn in the right place. Sometimes pressure groups try to get support for their ideas about where to draw the line by using the media to influence public opinion.

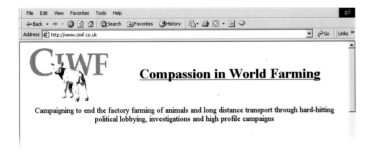

Campaigning to end the factory farming of animals and long distance transport through hard-hitting political lobbying, investigations and high profile campaigns

'Compassion in World Farming' is an example of a pressure group. The information below is taken from its website and explains how it began and what it tries to do.

The Beginning

Compassion in World Farming was started in 1967 by dairy farmer Peter Roberts. Peter and his wife Anna were becoming increasingly concerned with the animal welfare issues connected to the new systems of intensive farming that were becoming popular during the 1960s.

Unfortunately, at the time, Peter couldn't convince any of the major animal welfare societies to campaign against factory farming, but he was persuaded by a friend to do it himself and Compassion in World Farming was born.

Originally run from the Roberts family house, Compassion in World Farming has grown into an organisation with branches in Ireland, France and Holland and contacts throughout Europe and around the world.

Compassion in World Farming campaign through peaceful protest and lobbying and by raising awareness of the issue of farm animal welfare. We also produce fully referenced scientific reports. Our undercover team provide vital evidence of the suffering of farm animals. We have a wonderful network of supporters who help us in so many ways and celebrities who lend their time and support to our campaigns.

Our successes	
1987	Campaigning by CIWF leads to a phase-out of veal crates in the UK by 1990
1991	CIWF work with Sir Richard Body MP leads to the UK government introducing legislation to phase out sow stalls and tethers by 1999
1993	CIWF campaign on orphan lambs at market leads to new legislation being introduced
1996	Huge pressure from the UK and France results in an EU phase-out of veal crates by 2007
1997	CIWF's 10-year campaign to have animals recognised as Sentient Beings is successful
1999	CIWF's 30-year campaign to ban the battery cage results in an EU phase-out of battery cages
1999	Legislation to ban fur farming is tabled in the UK

Activities

1. How do you think it made a difference to Peter Roberts when he got other people to help him in his campaign against factory farming? In your answer show you have thought about:
   - what he would be able to do on his own
   - what he would be able to do when other people in the UK helped him
   - what he would be able to do once there were branches in Europe.

2. Some of the campaigns run by CIWF have lasted a long time before being successful. Why do you think Peter Roberts continued to fight for the cause even when he seemed to be making very little progress?

3. Why do you think it is important for CIWF to work with MPs?

Extension activity

4. Visit the Compassion in World Farming website
   - Choose one of the fact sheets and read the information.
   - Consider your own opinions on the issue.
   - Find a way to present all this information to your class. (You could use an ICT application to create your presentation.)

Getting technical

Lobby an attempt by an individual or a group to persuade a Member of Parliament to support their cause.

Parliament the group of people who are responsible for making laws. In this country most of them are elected.

Public opinion views held by people in general on the issues being considered by Parliament.

Sentient being a creature capable of feeling.

How are laws made?

In the UK, new laws are created by Parliament. This involves a lot of debate in both Houses of Parliament until all the details of the law are approved in a final vote. These two pages should help you to understand the process. They show how laws in general are formed.

 A

Before a law is passed, whilst it is still being discussed in Parliament, it is called a Bill.

H The Report Stage

The House discusses any changes that have been made to the Bill by the committee. At this point all the MPs have the opportunity to make further amendments.

I The Third Reading

This stage is usually quite short. The final form of the Bill is now voted on. If it is approved, it moves to the other House.

Getting technical

Civil servants people who do administrative work in a state department; they do not change when a new Government is elected.
By-law a regulation made by a local authority, for example a town council.

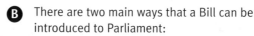

B There are two main ways that a Bill can be introduced to Parliament:
- by the Prime Minister's party (this is called a Government Bill)
- by any other MP (this is called a Private Member's Bill).

The diagrams on these two pages concentrate on how a Government Bill becomes Law.

G The Committee Stage

A smaller group of MPs from the different parties in the House discuss the Bill in more depth. They can suggest amendments (changes) to the content of the Bill.

J The House of Lords

The processes are more or less repeated in the Lords, except that the Committee Stage is done by the whole House. This means that the report stage is not needed. The Lords then take the final vote on the Bill.

C Before the Bill even reaches Parliament it needs to be written in rough, so the MPs will have something to work from. These draft Bills will be written by Civil Servants. At this time the Government might try to find out what public opinion is on the issue. It can do this by issuing a Green Paper, which is a document outlining some of the issues the Bill will cover, and asking for comment. Pressure groups often respond to these. Sometimes the Government issues a White Paper instead. This is a more definite statement of what the Government intends to do in a Bill.

D A Bill can start in either of the two Houses of Parliament. It is up to the Government to decide where it wants to begin the process. Usually, Bills begin in the House of Commons.

F **The Second Reading**

The main points of the Bill are discussed by all the MPs present in the House. The MPs then vote on whether to continue the process of making this Bill into a law. A majority of MPs need to vote in favour of this or the Bill will be dropped.

E **The First Reading**

The Government Minister who is responsible for the area of life the Bill will affect, reads out the title of the Bill. Often the title of a Bill is very long. There is no discussion of the Bill at this stage.

K If both Houses have agreed to the same Bill, then it is shown to the Monarch for Royal approval. In practice, this is never refused.

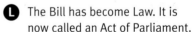

L The Bill has become Law. It is now called an Act of Parliament.

The time it takes for a Bill to become an Act of Parliament varies. It may take many months, but if it is something the Government thinks is important, it can take just a day.

Activities

1 If you were a member of a pressure group and you read something in a Green Paper you disagreed with, how might you show your concerns to the Government? Think of as many ways as you can.

2 Imagine there was a Bill called 'Scientific Procedures on Animals'.
- What do you think the Government would want to regulate through this legislation?
- Who might want to influence the outcome of the Bill? (Animal-rights activists? Cancer research scientists?)
- Try to find the names of some pressure groups from each side.
- Think about reasons for and reasons against using animals for scientific research.

How does Parliament debate an issue?

Every year Parliament spends hundreds of hours debating important issues. But what exactly is a debate? You might think that a debate is a free for all, with everyone shouting at once. In fact, a debate is a discussion which is run according to a certain set of rules.

All debates in Parliament begin with a motion. This is a statement setting out a focus for the debate so that the discussion does not become too general. In this way people can be clear about the decisions they are being asked to make. Because the motion is a specific statement, people have to decide whether they are in favour of it or against it. In practice this often depends on which political party they belong to. Parties usually have senior MPs called Whips. They tell members of their party which way to vote and tell off anyone who is not 'toeing the party line'.

Another way of ensuring a debate does not get out of hand is to have rules about what can be said when. The rules are similar in both Houses of Parliament but we are going to focus on the House of Commons.

The person who chairs the debate and ensures that things don't get out of hand is called the Speaker. This person is elected to the House as an MP, but when they are made Speaker they are not normally allowed to vote on any issues and they have to be impartial.

A debate normally begins with two MPs arguing in favour of the motion. It then continues with two others arguing against the motion. All these MPs are

Activities

1. Hold a debate following the method used in Parliament. You may wish to debate the motion 'This house believes that all testing of drugs on animals should be banned'. Remember, you will need:

    - a Speaker to chair the debate (this person must be impartial)
    - two main speakers for the motion
    - two main speakers against the motion
    - opportunities for other people to speak
    - permission to interrupt other speakers.

    You could arrange the classroom like the debating chamber in the House of Commons. It would be good if 2 or 3 pupils wrote notes on what happens as the debate proceeds.

normally Front Benchers (MPs who have been chosen by their Party Leaders to have special jobs). After this part of the debate, any other MPs who wish to contribute stand up to show they want to speak. Sometimes the person speaking allows this, but if they do not then the MP who made the interruption must sit down. If tempers rise and several MPs try to shout at once, the Speaker says 'Order, order' to bring the House back under control.

The debate ends with a summary speech by someone who is in favour of the motion. He or she ends the debate by replying to the arguments put forward by the opposition. The Speaker then asks the MPs to vote on the motion. This is first done verbally: MPs in favour shout 'Aye'; those against shout 'No'. Sometimes it is obvious which side wins the debate just by how loud they are. If it is not clear from this vote who has won, the Speaker will announce a Division.

A Division is when the MPs vote on an issue by walking through one of two doors into different rooms. The doors are marked 'Aye' and 'No'. MPs do not need to be in the debating chamber at the time to take part in the Division. A bell is rung throughout the House and MPs have eight minutes to register their vote. The people in each room are counted to see who has won the vote. Any MP who does not want to vote may abstain by staying in the debating chamber. If the vote is tied then the Speaker has a casting vote. The Speaker then announces the result by saying 'The Ayes [or Noes] have it'.

Activities

2 All debates in Parliament are recorded in a journal called *Hansard*. This is typed during the debate and printed overnight so MPs can read it the next day.

Imagine you are a *Hansard* reporter. Write a report of the debate you held in your classroom. Remember to record all the key events.

How is animal welfare of concern internationally?

Some issues are of concern not just to individuals or countries but to the world as a whole. They are a concern because their effects can be felt globally. This means that the environment or people in a different country from where the problem begins have to face the consequences of the situation.

Some international issues are connected with the welfare of people, others with the treatment of animals or the environment.

One concern is the ivory trade. In order to obtain the ivory from an elephant, the creature is killed. Even though the hunters are really after the oldest males because they have the best tusks, the way they hunt means that other elephants in a herd die as well.

Can you think of any other issues that are of international concern?

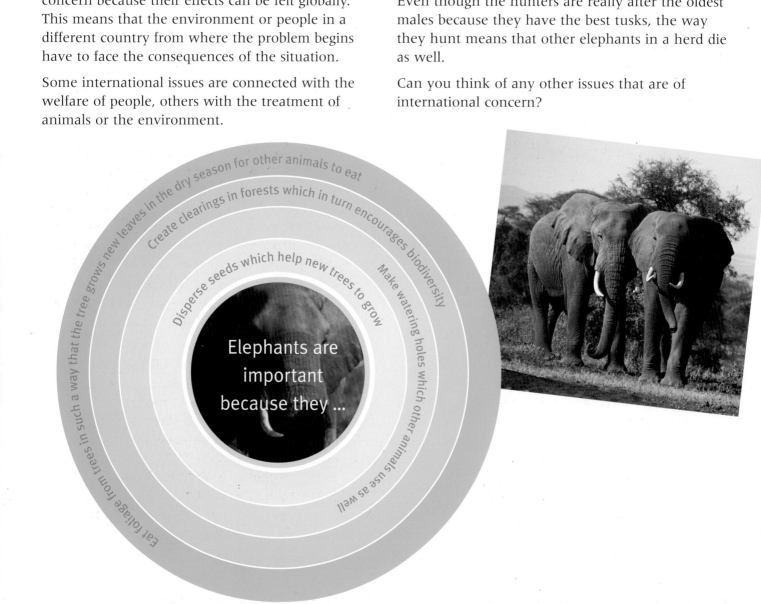

Elephants are important because they ...

Eat foliage from trees in such a way that the tree grows new leaves in the dry season for other animals to eat

Create clearings in forests which in turn encourages biodiversity

Disperse seeds which help new trees to grow

Make watering holes which other animals use as well

If elephants are killed without much care, the whole environment suffers. This means that countries have to think about controlling the hunting of elephants for the benefit of everyone. Even in the UK we have a responsibility to protect them, because what happens in other countries ultimately has an impact on us.

Individuals can help stop the trade in ivory by refusing to buy products that are made from it. However, to make a difference on a global scale, countries have to work together.

Countries that belong to CITES have agreed to put into action decisions made at the CITES conferences. Because CITES itself cannot make laws, the member countries have to make these agreements part of their own legislation.

It is not just representatives from the member countries who attend the conference. Although only these delegates can vote, others attend as observers and advisors. Amongst these delegates are people representing NGOs such as the World Wide Fund For Nature and TRAFFIC (the joint wildlife trade monitoring programme of WWF and IUCN – the World Conservation Union).

At the tenth CITES conference, held in Zimbabwe in 1997, there was a debate about whether some African countries should be allowed to start selling ivory (this had been banned in 1989). Some people argued that increased elephant numbers meant that it was now safe to allow a small amount of trade in ivory. Other people argued that all elephants still need to be protected. The conference decided that Namibia, Botswana and Zimbabwe could sell a small amount of ivory in a one-off sale.

These countries wish to be allowed to continue selling ivory, but at the eleventh CITES conference, held in Nairobi in 2000, it was decided that a total ban should remain in force. Although the UK does not have ivory to sell, it has to play a part in ensuring that the agreements made by CITES are enforced. One way it can do this is by seizing any ivory that is brought in to the UK illegally. The authority that does this is Customs and Excise, which is a department of the UK government.

Getting technical

NGO (Non-Governmental Organisation) a group that helps to enforce laws but is not itself part of any government. It is often an international body.

Treaty an agreement between countries about an issue and what should be done about it.

International organisation a pressure group that operates in different parts of the world.

International trade in animals is controlled by CITES (the Convention on International Trade in Endangered Species of Wild Fauna and Flora).

Activities

1. Write a letter to the UK delegates attending the next CITES conference, asking them either to continue to support the ban on the ivory trade or to vote for a relaxation of the restrictions. In your letter you should show that you know what has already been happening with the ivory trade since 1989 and that you have considered the different points of view.

2. Investigate the work of CITES in relation to another species (e.g. whales). You can find out about this by going to www.heinemann.co.uk/hotlinks and clicking on this activity.

Case study: the Hunting Bill

On 17 January 2001, MPs in the House of Commons were discussing a Bill about hunting with dogs. The debate lasted about four hours in total.

Below are some extracts from it. As you read them, you will see some real examples of the parliamentary procedure that was described on pages 42–43.

A

Parliament is the forum for debate on issues of public importance, and hunting with dogs is an issue on which the public have always shown interest, whether they are for or against it. Let that debate begin today.

Mr Mike O'Brien
(Under-Secretary of State for the Home Department)

B

My intention is to vote in favour of the first option – the self-regulation option. If that is defeated, I shall vote for the option of licensed hunting as second best. I intend to vote against the third option which proposes a complete ban on hunting with hounds.

Mr David Lidington *(MP for Aylesbury)*

C

Is the Honourable gentleman seriously telling the House that, in a democracy, the only means of expressing an opinion is to stand for election? There are pressure groups and organisations of every type ... but they do not all put forward candidates for election. The Countryside Alliance, like every other group, has every right to put its views in a democratic, fair and open way. It ill befits the Hon. gentleman to say that, because it has not proposed candidates for election, it is not a democratic organisation representing the views of many people in Britain.

Mr John Hayes *(MP for South Holland and the Deepings)*

D

Order. I remind Hon. Members to be brief. It is clear that many Members wish to contribute to the debate.

Madam Deputy Speaker

E

This has, in general, been a good, unemotional debate on an issue that arouses huge emotions. The emotions shown this evening have run less high than they did on Second Reading when we heard some quite intemperate language.

Mr James Paice *(MP for South-East Cambridgeshire)*

F

Since my election as an MP in 1997, I have received more correspondence on hunting than on any other issue ... The representations have been both for and against hunting. It is clearly an important issue to the constituents of all MPs, whatever their particular view. It might also be significant to members of the public because we have a free vote, which gives us the opportunity for once to act without the guidance of the Whips ... Because the issue is of concern to the public at large, and because we are to have a free vote, the onus is on us all to consider the issue properly.

Mr Norman Baker *(MP for Lewes)*

G

I spoke in the debate on 7 July on the Burns Report. It was a good and constructive debate. For me the Burns Report has clarified two important issues ...

Mr Caplin *(MP for Hove)*

H

As and when we vote in favour of Clause 3 tonight, as I think we will, may we have an undertaking from the Government that they will take the Bill forward on our behalf to the House of Lords and tell it that, if it does not act properly and democratically, as we will have done tonight, the Parliament Acts will be invoked and the Bill will be brought back here.

Mr Bill Etherington *(MP for Sunderland, North)*

I

The Bill has allowed all Hon. Members to have their say today and on Second Reading ... Without fear or favour, each of us must exercise his or her vote today ... I will exercise my judgement having read the Burns Report. I have considered my conscience on the views of liberty and cruelty. I will vote according to the sense of morality that the debate has given me. I will vote the way that I promised my constituents I would vote ... I now invite all Hon. Members to follow their consciences and to vote so that we can set out on the road by which this vexed issue will be resolved.

Mr Mike O'Brien
(Under-Secretary of State for the Home Department)

An anti-hunting protester is arrested

Activities

1 Using the knowledge you have gained from studying the rest of this chapter, answer the following questions.

a) Why did Mr Mike O'Brien begin and end the debate? (Quotes A and I)

b) Explain what is meant by (i) constituents and (ii) Whips in Quote F.

c) Read Quote B. Explain in your own words the three possible options that the MPs could vote for in this Bill.

d) Quotes G and I both refer to something called the Burns Report. What do you think this is, and why do you think the MPs thought it was so useful?

e) Look at Quotes D and E. Use them to explain why it is so important that parliamentary debates are chaired by a Speaker.

f) In Quote H, the MP talks about the Parliament Acts. From what you have learned about the progress of a Bill through Parliament, what do you think the Parliament Acts allow Parliament to do?

g) What is a 'free vote' in Parliament? (Quote F).

h) Why do you think this Bill had a free vote?

i) What do you think the MP who spoke before Mr Hayes (Quote C) said? Which do you think is the best way of trying to make or change laws: to belong to a pressure group or to be elected as an MP? Give reasons for your answer.

2 Some pressure groups use illegal forms of protest. Do you think this can ever be justified? Give reasons for your answer.

3 You have learned a lot in this chapter about how the laws that protect animals were made. You discovered that MPs commissioned an independent enquiry (the Burns Report) to find out the facts about hunting. This is because pressure groups on either side can be very biased. To see how, look at literature from The Countryside Alliance and The League Against Cruel Sports. Then complete a chart like the one here to show how each side has its arguments. You could use the website of each organisation. Go to www.heinemann.co.uk/hotlinks and click on this activity.

For hunting	Against hunting
Foxes are pests and must be controlled	Even if foxes are pests they should be shot rather than hunted with dogs

And finally...

Imagine you had been asked to choose the pictures for the first pages of this chapter. Make a list of what you would have chosen and why.

Chapter 4

The media and society

Learn about...

- How the media can be biased.
- The media in charity campaigns.
- How media reports can affect our views on sport.
- The individual's right to privacy.

A

D

E

B

F

C

Getting technical

Media the main means of mass communication.

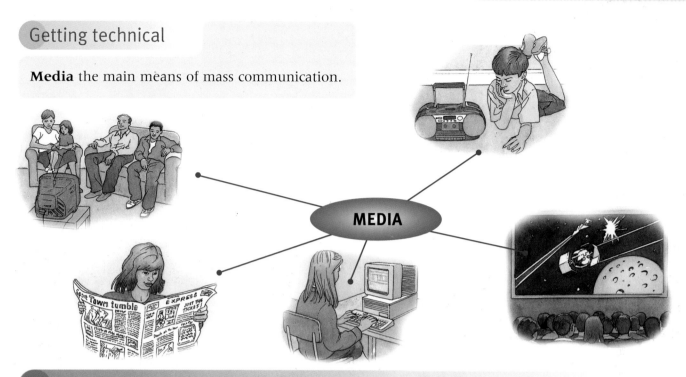

Activities

1. Start a word bank, using the names and definitions of the different forms of media.

2. Copy and complete the table below by inserting the following names and dates in the correct spaces:

Media	Developed by	Year
Film		
Internet		
Printing		
Radio		
Television		

Tim Berners-Lee, John Logie Baird, Johannes Gutenburg, Louis & Auguste Lumière, Guglielmo Marconi

1885   1896   1926   1989   1455

3. Draw a table and match the following companies to the correct media:

Freeserve	Columbia	Virgin	Carlton	The *Independent*
Heart	Universal	Anglia	AOL	*Daily Mail*

4. Use a CD-ROM to find out more about the inventors and their development of each aspect of the media.

5. Imagining you are one of the inventors named above, write a letter to a friend, explaining your invention.
What does it do and what can it be used for?
You can start with the writing frame below if you like.

> *Dear*
>
> *I have just invented a machine which ... , this means people will be able to ...*

How the media have changed our lives

● Living room in the 1930s

● Living room in the 1990s

Life before television

The account below describes how children in the 1930s might have spent their time.

After school if the weather was nice in the summer we would play in the streets, my sisters and I would play skipping, hide and seek or maybe hopscotch, sometimes we would even play whip and top. My brothers would play football or kick ball fly, sometimes we would all play rounders or marbles, or race on our skates. On Fridays and Saturday mornings my eldest brother had a job delivering groceries for the local shop. Occasionally the whole family would go for a walk together.

If the weather was bad or in winter we would stop in and listen to the radio, two of our favourite programmes were 'In Town Tonight' and 'The Riddle of the Sands', or we might just sit around and read a comic. Other nights we would have friends round, my sisters and I would play on the piano with our friends and my brothers would swap their cigarette cards with their friends. Other times we would all play games together, cards, dominoes, snakes and ladders or ludo.

Sometimes at weekends if a good film was showing my parents would let us all go to the pictures to the Saturday matinée.

Time (hours)	No. of pupils
0	2
0–1	10
1–2	9
2–3	22
3–4	1
More than 4	6

● 1990s: pupils' television viewing statistics (one evening for 14-year-old pupils)

Activities

At home: ask your parents and grandparents how they used to spend their time at home when they were young.

1. Does the media reflect or affect society? Many people believe that violence in the media affects people's behaviour, especially that of children. One report claimed that television was the strongest single contributing factor in making the world more violent. Similarly with teenagers and sex, one report claims that the 'key to the increase in sexual activity among young people was the media'. The report went on to suggest that the 'macho' message in men's magazines implied that 'if you're not having sex there's something wrong with you'. In small groups, discuss the impact of media on society. In groups, discuss this information and statement.

2. Use the Internet to find other articles that suggest how the media affect society.

3. Discuss the differences between pictures A and B.

4. Carry out a television-viewing survey for your class and plot the results as a graph.

5. What is the main difference between how children spent their time in the 1930s and how they spend their time now? Discuss how this difference might be affecting children's development.

6. Today television soaps are a very popular type of programme. Why do you think this is?

7. Try to work out the names of the following soaps:

   aafmirffyalis   mwydoanhaae   grnheosiub   scerooteittnnaro   sssoorrcad

Extension activity

8. Write a short script for a popular television soap.

The media and the news

● Front page of a broadsheet newspaper

For thousands of years news was passed on by word of mouth or in letters.

In Europe after the invention of printing, news was circulated on 'broadsheets'. These were printed on one side only and contained no pictures or headlines.

● A television newsreader

● Internet news website

Sputnik 1, the first artificial satellite, was launched by the USSR in 1957.

Following the launch of *Sputnik 1*, the development of satellite technology has allowed news from around the world to be relayed live into our homes.

At home watch the evening television news for a week and listen to the radio news. Do you think it is mostly fair reporting?

● Sputnik 1

Bias in the media

The media can create a biased impression in many ways, for example, by only giving one side of a story, or by using extreme language to exaggerate one aspect of a story. There are many reasons why the media might want to create a biased view. It could be to attract people's interest and boost sales, or to promote the political views of the companies' owners or senior executives. Some media companies in Britain are accused of producing articles that are biased towards one particular political party. In its most extreme case, bias in media controlled by the government is called propaganda.

Now read this Internet news article:

● Greg Dyke

Tories watch for BBC bias

The Conservative Party has appointed media monitors to scour BBC output for political bias after Greg Dyke's controversial appointment as the next director-general.

The Tories were furious that Mr Dyke was chosen by BBC governors, who knew he had donated £55,000 to the Labour Party in recent years.

Mr Dyke has now severed links with the party, and insists he will defend the corporation's reputation for independence. He will take the post in April.

Tory leader William Hague has already made his protest known by writing to the chairman of the Board of Governors, Sir Christopher Bland.

Activities

1. Satellites have speeded up other things besides the reporting of news items. Discuss other ways in which satellites have affected media communications.

2. Does the use of satellites have a good effect on the media? (Is it useful to see starving people or bombings on news items?)

3. Why do you think the Tory party thought the BBC might produce biased reports?

4. Why is it important for the BBC not to produce biased programmes?

Refugees flooding into UK like ants

● *Daily Express*, 7 November 2001

Getting technical

Bias the representation of facts more to one side of a story than another.

Left wing media that support the Labour Party and represent socialist values.

Right wing media that support the Conservative Party and represent conservative values.

Broadsheet in the past, a single sheet of paper with the news printed on one side; now, a style of newspaper containing financial and business information printed on a full page.

Tabloid a popular style of newspaper with bold headlines and large pictures printed on half-size pages.

Propaganda opinions or principles, especially biased ones, that are spread in order to persuade or change people's minds.

The facts about refugees entering Britain can be found on the Refugee Council website.

The figures tell a different story to the one suggested by the newspaper article above. In 2001, 71 700 asylum applications from refugees were made in the UK. That's 11% less than in 2000. In 2001, far from being the top destination, the UK ranked 12th in the EU in terms of applications from refugees.

However, this is not the impression given in newspaper articles like the one above. That article suggests that the UK is the only destination for refugees. It also uses emotional language, such as 'flooding' and 'ants' to express its views about refugees.

Activities

1 Read the information at the top of page 53. How can the media create a biased image? Why do some media companies produce biased articles?

2 Read the newspaper headline A above, then read the facts from the Refugee Council. Is the headline correct? Which simile is used to create a biased image?

Extension activity

3 Find some examples of headlines that you think are biased. How would you rewrite them to give a less biased image?

4 Further articles on refugees entering Britain can be found by going to www.heinemann.co.uk/hotlinks and clicking on this activity. Look at this website and analyse it for bias.

How can media advertising influence sales?

The first Coca Cola advertisement was produced in 1886 in the USA. Within ten years Coke was being drunk in every state in America and today its logo is recognised around the world. Companies now spend billions of pounds on advertising their products in the media in the hope of influencing our choice of products. Advertising agencies use many different strategies to attract our attention and encourage us to buy the products they are advertising.

Some of these different strategies are illustrated in the adverts included below.

A

C

D

B # 50% OFF
Selected items in this store

E
You can't buy better!

F ## The New Ralfa Supremo
Does 0–60mph in 1 second!
Best ever car, guaranteed

The Advertising Standards Authority is the regulatory authority for non-broadcast advertisements in the UK. It is responsible for monitoring and maintaining the standard of adverts in magazines and newspapers, on posters and billboards, in direct mail and new media (e.g. internet adverts, commercial email and text message adverts). The authority administers the British Codes of Advertising and Sales Promotion to ensure that adverts are legal, decent, honest and truthful. Two examples from its advertising code are:

- All advertisements should be legal, decent, honest and truthful.

- All advertisements should be prepared with a sense of responsibility to consumers and to society.

More of the Advertising Standards code can be seen by going to the ASA's website– see activity 3, below.

The new anti-ageing face cream from *Pierre Laurent*
Guaranteed to make your skin ten years younger in a week!

Getting technical

Advert a means of displaying information about goods or services.

Endorsement a declaration of approval of goods or services.

Logo an emblem used as a badge by a company or product.

Slogan a short, catchy phrase used in advertising.

Activities

1. Discuss the strategies used in adverts A to E on page 55. Can you think of other strategies that adverts use?

2. Discuss why proposed adverts F and G might provoke complaints.

3. Many adverts encourage child 'pester power'. What do you think this means, and is it an acceptable way of selling things? Write four rules of your own which you think should apply to adverts. Next, you might like to compare your rule to those given by the Advertising Standards Authority. Go to www.heinemann.co.uk/hotlinks and click on this activity.

4. Cut out an image of a product and scan the image into the computer. Now write an advert for your product, including a slogan.

5. Match these stars to the product they endorse:

David Beckham	Jamie Oliver	Britney Spears	Elton John	Ivana Trump
Royal Mail	Kentucky Fried Chicken	Pepsi	Brylcream	Sainsbury's

6. Next, discuss these two questions about celebrity endorsements:
   - Do the celebrities use the products they endorse?
   - Do the celebrities have the ability to make informed recommendations?

How are campaigns developed through the media?

Singer Bob Geldof was watching a BBC television report in October 1984, about the starving people of Ethiopia. The programme brought home the horror people were facing as their crops failed, and he decided to try to do something to help. First, he organised the recording and release of the Band Aid single 'Do they know it's Christmas?'. It raised approximately £8 million. In the following year, he organised the Live Aid concerts in London and Philadelphia, which raised approximately £100 million.

A

B

C

- Charity donations for the year 2000/01

Worldwide Fund for Nature	£74 million*
Children in Need	£18 million
Comic Relief	£23 million
Save the Children	£97.3 million*
RSCPA	£17.9 million*

*These funds represent a year's worth of fund-raising events

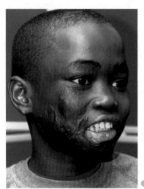

- Issa Kamara

WIN £250 TODAY!

What's on your TV

The stars of Brookenders!

5.30pm Pudsey Bear sings

6pm Special report on Hayley, a little girl helped by Children in Need last year

On TV tonight

7pm	Brookenders – will Joe marry Rita?
7.30pm	The Animal Wildlife programme
8.30pm	Crime everywhere! Catch a robber special
9pm	News
10pm	Celebrity Singalong for Children in Need
10.30pm	Children in Need update special
11.30pm	Comedy for Children in Need

Should the media take up the cause of individuals?

During the summer of 2001, the *Eastern Daily Press* in Norwich raised the money for Issa Kamara, who had been tortured during Sierra Leone's civil war, to be brought to Britain to receive medical treatment. Initially it was said that NHS rules wouldn't allow the treatment to go ahead. However, after Issa's plight was raised on national radio and newspapers, the go-ahead was given for Issa to come to Britain for the necessary medical treatment.

Activities

1. Which charity organisation was established by Sir Bob Geldof? How did he become aware of the need for this charity?

2. Look at images A and C on page 57. Which organisation does each represent? What does each organisation do with its money? How do the images help to raise money for the charity?

3. Look at the table of funds raised by each charity at the top of this page. Draw a graph of these figures. How do the media affect the money raised by some charities?

4. Read about Issa Kamara, then discuss the role of the media in raising money for the treatment of sick children.

5. Visit the websites for the charities covered on page 57. Find out about the work they do and how they raise their money.

6. Use the Internet to find out about the fund-raising event Net Aid, or about SportsAid.

How do the media portray sports and their supporters?

The media today have a tremendous influence on sports. The high levels of media coverage given to some sports personalities can enable them to become 'superstars' earning millions of pounds a year from sponsorship deals alone. However, in some cases the media can destroy the careers of people involved in sports, especially football managers, who can be forced to leave their jobs due to the criticism they receive in the media.

Do you agree that the media should be able to force changes of football managers using headlines like this?

Keegan suffers the odd goal in seven

Now look at the media sports images A to E.

Sports personality quiz

For each of the people in these photographs, conduct a class survey, using the following questions:

- What is this person's name?
- Which sport do they represent?
- What is their highest achievement?

'Arrogant, like Liverpool in the Eighties'

I was as at the Southampton–Manchester United game with my two sons when four United thugs were arrested and marched away by the police.

The contempt shown by some United fans away from home is appalling. Some refuse to sit, which causes the law-abiding element to stand so they can watch the game. Stewards then, quite rightly, ask all of the fans to sit down.

This is twisted around by the United fans and reported as 'over-enthusiastic' stewarding.

These so-called fans are arrogant and confrontational. Unfortunately, there is an element in United's support who believe they can do what they want. They are rather like Liverpool fans in the Eighties, arrogant in the extreme with scant regard for anyone else.

● Letter sent to the *Daily Mail* (9/8/01)

Activities

1 Look at images A to E on page 59, then discuss the following questions:
- Is the image positive or negative?
- What effect do negative images have on sports?
- What might be the cause of the high levels of hooligan behaviour associated with some sports? How much is the behaviour on the pitch (image E) a factor? Or the media coverage (image C)?

2 Look at image A. What is happening? What effect might this image have on the level of interest in this sport?

3 Which of the three sports stars in the quiz did most pupils know? With a partner, discuss why some sports stars are more famous than others. Use the Internet to find out more about the achievements of the stars. Then as a class, discuss which of the three stars has achieved the most. Write your own script for a news report on the achievements of one sports star.

4 Look at the pie charts below. For each newspaper, answer the following questions:
- Which sport gets most coverage?
- Which sport gets least coverage?

If you like, you could use the following writing frame:
The *Daily Express* gives most coverage to ... and it gives least coverage to ... *The Times* newspaper gives most coverage ... and it gives least coverage to ...

5 Why do you think some sports get less coverage than others?

6 Why do you think some papers give more coverage to some sports than others?

7 At home, read the sports pages of your daily newspaper. Do you think they are fair and unbiased?

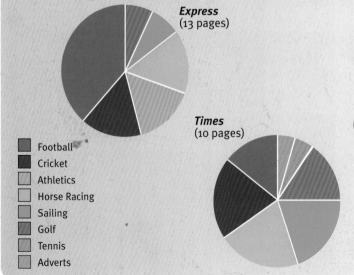

Express (13 pages)

Times (10 pages)

- Football
- Cricket
- Athletics
- Horse Racing
- Sailing
- Golf
- Tennis
- Adverts

Extension activity

8 Read the letter 'Arrogant, like Liverpool in the Eighties', then answer the following questions:
- What is the writer's impression of the United fans?
- Which words give this impression?
- What effect do you think these fans might have on the writer's support for football?
- How do you think his two sons felt at the match?

Should celebrities have the same right to privacy as everyone else?

The right to privacy is considered a basic human right to which all people are entitled. In Britain it is protected by the 1998 Human Rights Act:

Article 8
Everyone has the right to respect for private and family life, home and correspondence.

The media, however, often argue that they have a right to print information under the same Human Rights Act that protects the freedom of the Press.

Article 10
Everyone has the right to freedom of expression.

Pictures and articles about famous individuals are of interest to the public, but is it acceptable to expose the inappropriate or illegal actions of the individual concerned?

A
● Lord Archer faces paparazzi on his way to court

● A celebrity facing the massed ranks of paparazzi

B
● Before his family skiing holiday, Prince Charles often appears before the cameras for a photo session

C

Getting technical

Paparazzi photographers who follow celebrities, trying to get photographs of them to sell to newspapers or magazines

Activities

1 Look at images A, B and C on page 61. What do you think is happening? Is there a difference between the role of the photographers in the three images?

2 Why do you think newspapers buy paparazzis' photographs of celebrities? Should celebrities be protected from these photographs being taken?

3 On 24 September 2001, Prince William was photographed meeting the crowd in St Andrews. Why do you think he did this?

4 Consider the two case studies below. For each one, decide if the individual's privacy had been invaded.

Case study 1

A footballer who did not want the press to release the story of his secret affairs.

Case study 2

Photographs of an individual attending and leaving a Drugs Anonymous meeting were published, after that individual had previously denied using drugs.

Extension Activity

5 In 1994 the *Sun* newspaper published articles accusing footballer Bruce Grobellar of match-fixing. This was based on a video tape of a meeting in a hotel room at which Bruce Grobellar was offered money to fix match results.
Was this good investigative journalism or an invasion of privacy?

6 Should exposing criminal behaviour be left to the police?
Use the Internet to find out what happened in this case. Go to www.heinemann.co.uk/hotlinks and click on this activity.

Review and reflect

In this chapter you have looked at how the media here changed people's lifestyle by bringing entertainment into the home through television. You have also considered the influence the media have on modern culture through advertising, for example by creating fashion trends which everyone, especially the young, are under pressure to follow.

You have looked at the media's effects on people's thoughts and attitudes through up-to-the-minute news reports and media campaigns. You have also considered the effect the media can have through biased reporting and the invasion of individuals' privacy.

As an MP, you cannot expect your home life to stay private, especially if you break the law.

When you are a film star, the public are interested to know about the life you lead, how you spend your holidays, where you go, what you do.

Activity

1. In pairs, discuss the two statements above. Do you agree with them, or disagree? Explain your answers.

Review and reflect

Activities

1. Draw a spider diagram of what you have learned in this chapter.

2. Here are some opinions about the media. Discuss them and and decide if you agree with them or not.
   - The media have made the world a smaller place.

   - Violence on television is reflected in children's behaviour.

   - Health magazines create low self esteem.

3. Complete your word bank with the rest of the new words you have covered in this topic. Include a definition for each word.

4. Classify the following as either positive or negative influences of the media:
   - reports of starvation in Africa
   - fashion advertising
   - coverage of hooliganism at sporting events
   - investigation of MPs' dishonest actions
   - real-life drama soaps
   - media coverage giving some footballers superstar status

   Add further examples of your own which represent negative and positive influences of the media.

5. Using all the information covered in this topic, prepare a short presentation on the question: How do the media affect the lives of people today?

Chapter 5

How can we make decisions?

Learn About...

- How group decisions are made.
- How to hold a successful meeting.
- How to communicate with different members of your community.
- How to recognise a good leader.
- How to hold an election.

Imagine what it would be like if no one listened to your opinion about things that affected your life. You would have to eat exactly what other people decided to eat, go or stay wherever others wanted to all the time, be with people you did not like, or be alone when you might want company. You would be no better off than a prisoner or a slave in that group!

But how can we affect group decisions that might change our lives? This unit will help you to think about how we might make group decisions.

In ancient Greece, people would gather in the market places to discuss issues that affected them all. Then they would vote on what to do, and the most popular choice would be acted upon. This way of deciding things became known as democracy, which means 'rule by the people'. The people (apart from slaves and women) would decide on what should happen.

● Slaves

● Discussions in a Greek marketplace

● The Houses of Parliament

Activities

① In pairs, brainstorm a short list of things that you would like to change about the world around you. You might include:
- a change in school
- a change in how the 'over-11s' are treated
- a change in your community
- a good cause that needs support.

② Pick a good idea that you can both agree on, and share it with the rest of the class.

③ Now imagine that your class has the chance to support only one of the ideas, and to see if it can be put into practice. In groups of four or five, discuss the best way for the class to decide which one gets picked. You might want to think about:
- What different ways of choosing there might be.
- Which ways are going to be fair to everyone.
- Who is going to decide. Everyone? The teacher? Just a few people?
- Who is going to organise the decision-making process? Why them?
- Is there time for everyone to be listened to? If not, is there a solution to this problem?

④ Choose a representative for your group. Report back to the class on what your group thought was the best way to make a decision.

⑤ As a class, agree (if you can!) on how you will choose the idea you will support.

⑥ Now make the decision! Which idea was chosen?

⑦ Do you think everyone in the class will be satisfied with the result? Say why or why not. (Is it possible to please everyone all the time?)

⑧ Write down any thoughts about how group decisions should be made. Are there any rules you would make?

Getting technical

Democracy 'rule by the people'; a way of making decisions where the people involved have a say in what happens.

How can 60 000 000 people make fair decisions together?

You may have discovered that there can be many ways to make a decision as a group of people. A decision might be made, for example, by:

- a single ruling or trusted person in the group
- a few chosen people in the group
- everyone in the group
- someone outside the group.

Can you think of examples in school where these different ways of making decisions are happening? (Think about sports teams, the headteacher, or different groups of teachers or pupils.) Why do you think these different ways are used in the different situations?

If making decisions as a class is difficult, just imagine the problems of getting the whole UK population (about 60 000 000 people) to make them! Obviously, it would be difficult for everyone to take part in every decision that needs to be made. It would cost billions of pounds, and there wouldn't be any time to do anything else! So, a type of democracy is used where the people still have an effect on the decisions made (rule by the people), but they elect (choose) by ballot certain individuals to represent them, or speak on their behalf instead. It is called a representative democracy. It is useful because a small group of people can speak on behalf of a much larger number, making it easier to debate ideas and make decisions.

In the UK, these elected people, or 'representatives', gather at the Houses of Parliament in London to debate issues and vote on them for us. They are called Members of Parliament (MPs), and there are 659 of them. They are elected every five years by people over 18 who live in the 659 different areas (or constituencies) that the UK has been divided into.

Getting technical

Representative democracy a system that enables a large number of people to make decisions by choosing a smaller number of people to speak on their behalf.

Elect to choose, usually by voting for someone in an election.

Ballot a way of voting where people can make their choices privately.

Debate one way of arguing about two sides of an issue, and reaching a decision about it.

MP Member of Parliament. Someone chosen to speak on behalf of the people who elected them in their constituency.

Constituency in the UK, one of 659 areas, each represented by an MP.

Representative someone who is chosen to speak on behalf of their group.

Activities

1. Find out the name of your constituency. Go to www.heinemann.co.uk/hotlinks and click on this activity.

2. Can you find out who your local MP is? What is his or her name?

3. Are there any school decisions that are made in the same way as a representative democracy? Is there anyone who you voted for in your school to speak on your behalf? Jot the details down.

4. Do you think everyone over the age of 10 should be able to vote for their choice of MP? Why is that a good, or a bad, idea?

● MPs are elected by people living in their constituency

How can meetings be made more effective?

Making decisions as a group is a bit like playing in a sports team. If the team members work hard together and communicate well, they will achieve a good result. If they argue a lot, or don't co-operate with each other, then the result can be a disaster! This unit will help you work out how to hold a successful meeting.

Start by thinking of any meetings that you know about or take part in. Are there any team meetings, or meetings in school, or with people from your local area? Why do they happen and how are they organised?

● Meetings, like team games, need their members to work well together to achieve success

Activities

1 The class should divide into two groups. One half will present a drama of 'a meeting that goes extremely well'. The other half will present 'a meeting that goes very badly'. The meetings should be held for about 10–15 minutes, and should aim to 'recommend fair punishments for bullies to the headteacher'.
Here are some things for both groups to think about:

a) Who is going to:
- keep time so that the aim is completed by the end of the meeting?
- decide the agenda? (How the aim can be achieved step by step.)
- who speaks when, and for how long? (Would having a chairperson help?)
- keep a record of what happens during the meeting? (A secretary?)

b) What skills does everyone need to:
- make sure that everyone who wants to speak gets a chance to speak?
- build on each other's ideas?
- work together?
- make sure that disagreements are about an idea and not 'personal'?
- help each other listen to one person at a time?
- make the meeting friendly, but avoid wasting time?
- allow decision-making to be fair?

2 Prepare your meeting plans as a group. You don't have to write every word that people will say, just plan the key events and a few scenes within it. Make the rest up as you go along.

3 While each half of the class presents its 'meeting', make a few notes on things that helped it go well or badly. Think about:
- people's attitudes
- timing
- the aim of the meeting
- how people worked together (examples?)
- how the meeting was 'chaired' (run by the chairperson).

4 Compare the two meetings in a class discussion. What did they tell you about meetings? (Can you use any of the 'good meeting' skills in your discussion?!)

5 List 'Six golden rules for a successful meeting'.

Getting technical

Chairperson the person who organises and runs or 'chairs' the meeting.

Secretary the person who makes a record of what is decided during the meeting.

Agenda a list of things to be dealt with during the meeting.

Case study

Bob Geldof watched a news programme on TV in 1984 and it changed the future for him and millions of others. The programme described how millions of people were starving to death in Africa, and how many more were going to die if they didn't get help very soon. The pictures were terrible, and it really made him want to do something about it.

Less than a couple of months later a single was released called 'Do they know it's Christmas?' by Band Aid. Many of the best pop stars featured on it, and it became the best selling British record of its time, raising £8 000 000 which was used to send food and aid to Africa. Today, the money raised has risen to about £50 000 000, and has been used to save countless lives.

Everyone can have great ideas like Bob, but putting them into practice is another challenge altogether. Bob could not have raised so much support or money on his own. He had to get other people involved, so he created a campaign (or a series of activities) to get their support and raise the money. Without communication, Bob's campaign would never have been able to start, and the people in Africa would not have been saved.

Getting technical

Campaign a series of activities that aim to achieve a goal.

1 Imagine you have an idea that you want people in school to know about. Perhaps it's to raise money for a charity, or to organise a talent show, or to start a new after-school club. What could you do to let people know about it and get their support? Brainstorm in small groups to see how many ways of communicating you can think of.

Think about communicating ...

• in writing or signs (notice boards, posters? What else? Where?)
• in spoken words (assemblies?)
• with pupils: form or year groups, a school council?
• with adults: teachers, other staff, the staff-room notice board?

3 Is there anything in school that you would like to change, or draw people's attention to? Use that idea, or imagine being Bob Geldof trying to set up Live Aid, and design a poster, postcard, large cartoon, placard or 'symbol with slogan' which would tell people about it.

4 Why not try your idea out? Bob did (now he's Sir Bob Geldof!). You never know what you might achieve and who might help!

Think about:

• What are the most important details to communicate on your sign?
• Where would it go?
• Who are you trying to communicate with?
• How could people find out more or get back to you?

2 Join with one or two other groups, and hold a meeting to decide on which ideas to use. (Remember what you learned in the 'Meeting' on page 68.)

Getting technical

Slogan phrase or catchwords used in politics or advertising.

Placard large board with a slogan on it, carried in public for people to see.

Of course, you are part of other communities as well as school! What if you wanted to change something like local bus services, or how old people are treated in your county, or how animals are transported in England, or how polluted the world is? How and who would you communicate with then?

Activities

1 Think of one thing that people might want to change in these different areas:

a) the local community (e.g. a local town)
b) a country (e.g. England)
c) a continent (e.g. Europe)
d) the world.

2 Use the information below to investigate how you might be able to have your opinions heard.

Communicating through the media

The word 'media' refers to the ways in which information can be communicated to the public. TV or radio programmes, newspapers, magazines, or websites, for example, are all forms of media. Your opinions can reach a lot of people through the media, but you usually need to do or know something that the media people (like reporters) think the public would like to know about.

Communicating with the Government

The Government makes decisions that affect the country, and it's made up of Members of Parliament who can speak on your behalf at Government meetings. You can contact your local MP to give your views on local or national (country) issues. See if you can find out who your local MP is, and how to contact him or her. Go to www.heinemann.co.uk/hotlinks and click on this activity.

Communicating with the local community

Sometimes you may want to change something only in your area. Better local transport? A safe play area for young people? Your local council is made up of councillors who have been locally chosen (or elected) to look after local services and any problems that might arise. You can communicate with them by contacting your local library for the address, or find them on the internet using a search engine.

You could also join a local group or go to local meetings involved with the area that you want to change.

A local council meeting

An MP addressing the public

3 Describe in your own words what the media, the government and the local council are, and briefly describe how you could contact them.

4 **Communicate your ideas!**
As a class, hold a meeting to decide:

- What to communicate. (What would you like to change or make people aware of?)
- Who to communicate with. (The public? The government? The local council? Which would be best for your idea?)
- Vote for one or two people to do the writing for you.
- Have a more detailed discussion with them so that they can represent accurately what you want to say.
- When they have written it, make sure they tell you what they have written before they send it so that you can all agree on what it says.

Getting technical

Local council a group of people who have been elected to make decisions about the local community.

Media ways of communicating with the public (TV, radio, newspapers, websites, magazines, etc.).

How am I represented at my school?

Do you know if anyone is speaking for you in your school? (If you don't, perhaps you should find out, or find someone who will!) Who are they? Do they really know what to say on your behalf? How can they find out your opinions? Are they a good person for the job? This unit will help you to answer these questions.

Is someone speaking for me?

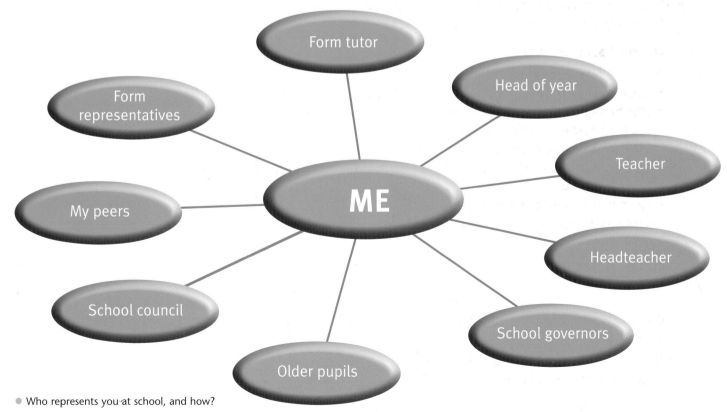

- Who represents you at school, and how?

Activities

What kind of person should represent me?

What kinds of skills or qualities should a representative have?

Which ones are really important, and which ones would be helpful, but not necessary?

Imagine you are in the two groups (a form, and a sports team) in the table below. Which qualities or skills would you want your representative for each group to have? Copy out the table below and give each quality a score out of ten showing how important they are or not (10 = very important, 0 = not important at all). You could fill in the last column yourself, for your qualities and skills, or get a friend to do it!

Quality or skill	Form Representative	Sports team captain	You!
Honest			
Humorous			
Determined			
Fit and healthy			
Lively and loud			
Good at listening			
Good at speaking			
Creates ideas			
Popular			
Reliable			
Good leader			
Fair			
Organised			
(Add your own idea here)			

1 Did the Form Rep and the sports team captain have exactly the same scores? Try to explain any differences that you notice to a neighbour. Did they agree with your scoring?

2 What qualities or skills did you score best on?

3 Pick one of your own lower scores. What could you do to improve it?

4 List the 'top five' qualities or skills that you and your neighbour think that a good representative should have. Compare these to the rest of the class. Find out why people agreed or disagreed on them.

5 Briefly describe actions that would show that someone had your top five qualities or skills (for example, 'I could tell someone was reliable because they always turn up to team practice on time').

What makes a good leader?

A representative's job is to represent the views of the people who elected them. A leader, however, is slightly different. Their job is to lead or direct a group of people in the right direction as they see it, as well as to listen to the opinions of their group. Your headteacher could be seen as a 'leader' of the school.

Activities

1. What other leaders can you think of, and what qualities or skills do they have? (Think of teams, political parties, the Government, people from history, etc.)

2. Think of some famous people. Choose two who would make excellent leaders, and two who would not. What would they be leaders of?

3. **School display!**
   Design a large display for a wall in your school, showing what skills or qualities a good representative or good leader should have.

4. Knowing what kind of person should represent you is a good start, but what if other people disagree with your choice? What is a fair way for everyone to choose a single person to represent their group?

This unit should have helped you understand how elections work, and allowed you to choose a form representative for your school council or year group in a real election.

Think!

A general election is when voters can decide on who should run the government of this country. It happens every five years. Can you remember any images or ideas from the general election in May 2001?

One type of election process:

1 Everyone votes in private for their choice of form representative (this is called a secret ballot).

2 The four people who got the most votes are now candidates (or possibilities) for being form representative (if they agree!).

3 Candidates might want to make a short speech telling the voters (or electorate) why they would be good at representing them. (How would they hear your views? Have they proof of skills or qualities that a good representative should have?)

4 Hold the election! A second secret ballot is held to decide which one of the four candidates should become form representative.

5 The votes are counted, and the result is announced.

Getting technical

Secret ballot a private vote where no one else knows how you voted. In 16th-century Venice, people made their vote known by placing a small ball in a box. The Italian for 'small ball' is ballotta!

Candidate someone who is standing for election.

Electorate people who have the right to vote.

School council a group of teachers and pupils who meet to discuss issues and ideas about school. Pupils in the council are elected by their peers from different year groups or forms. The school council is one important way for the views of pupils to be heard.

Activities

1 You may choose to hold this election for real, or decide to hold a 'mock election'.

2 What changes might be made to the election process? Would it be any different if:
   a) Elections were held every month, every three months, or once a year? How?
   b) Each voter got two votes to use instead of one in the election? (Try it!)
   c) There were only two candidates allowed, not four?
   d) The ballot (or vote) was not secret, but took place in front of everyone else?

So, how are you represented?

1 Who does the form representative meet with?

2 How often?

3 How could you make sure they get to know your opinions?

4 How do they communicate what happens in the meetings to you?

5 What other ways are you represented in school? Think about:
- talking to teachers (form tutors)
- talking to pupils in higher year groups
- parents' evenings
- school newsletters or website
- notice boards / clubs / assemblies.

● Having a secret ballot means no one can know how you voted

● As the winning candidate in his constituency, this person is now one of the UK's 659 MPs

Review and reflect

This chapter has been about 'developing your skills of democratic participation' or 'how to take part in making decisions well as a group'. You have learned about:

- The different ways and situations in which group decisions can be made.
- How to hold meetings well.
- The different ways in which views can be communicated.
- How your views can be shared in your school by representatives or leaders.

If you don't try to change things, have you any right to complain?

Activities

You have also tried out some of these things for yourselves, and have seen how they are carried out locally and nationally. So, how much have you learned? Try these challenges to give yourself an idea of your own progress:

1 In your own words, write down what the following words mean:
   a) democracy
   b) representative
   c) Member of Parliament
   d) constituency
   e) debate
   f) student council
   g) election
   h) campaign
   i) ballot.

2 In pairs or small groups, describe one way in which you could solve the following problem 'step by step':
900 people live in Spaghettiville. The roads there are dangerous and need to be sorted out urgently. Unfortunately, there isn't time to listen to everyone's views. How can the community work out what to do in a fair and swift way?

3 If you were advising a new chairperson about holding a successful meeting, what five (short) pieces of advice would you give them?

4 Imagine that you discover that a local factory is polluting your local river. Dead fish can be seen floating in it, and people who swim or canoe in it start to get ill. How could you stop the pollution? Who could you communicate with, and how would you communicate?

5 Other year groups don't seem to notice that the Year 7 playground and toilet area are for Year 7 only! What could the Year 7s do to reclaim their area?

6 Having used this chapter, pick at least four statements that you really agree with from the list below, and two that you would like to improve on:
   a) I participated (took part) in making a group decision.
   b) I listened to others carefully.
   c) I suggested some ideas of my own to others.
   d) I spoke clearly and made myself understood.
   e) I used different methods of communicating my ideas.
   f) I learned more about how people make decisions in the country.
   g) I found out what my local constituency is, and who my MP is.
   h) I learned at least four new words and their meanings.
   i) I now know how to take part in a meeting.
   j) I have made more of a difference to my community / school.

7 How could you make progress in the two areas that you would like to improve? Make a plan and act on it!

CONGRATULATIONS! Well done with your progress! If you would like to know more about how you can change the world around you and make sure that your voice is heard, why not try these websites for more ideas and information? Go to www.heinemann.co.uk/hotlinks and click on these activities.

a) for MP, political party and constituency information

b) teenagers who have campaigned and volunteered; information, advice and examples

c) advice and information about elections.

Chapter 6

Developing your school grounds

Learn about...

Your school grounds are sometimes the only large open space in a neighbourhood, and form an important part of the local community. However, they are often under-used and could be developed in a more sustainable way. In this unit you will learn about:

- Planning and carrying out ways of improving your school grounds.

- How to undertake a survey of the school grounds.

- How to analyse your findings.

- Developing plans to meet the school's needs and those of the local community.

- Recognising the importance of discussing and balancing the needs of different people.

- Carrying out and taking part in an agreed plan for improvement.

A survey of your school grounds

You are going to use your skills of observation and recording in order to fill in two simple survey sheets. You could also collect extra evidence using a digital camera or even a video camera.

● Survey 1 - How the school grounds are currently used during the day

Time of day	Areas used	Activities
Before school starts		
Breaktime		
Lunchtime		
During lessons		
After school		
At weekends		

● Survey 2 - The needs of different groups that use the grounds

Group	What they need
PE teachers	
Other teachers	
Pupils at the school	
Community groups	
Adult learning groups	
Sports clubs	

Activities

1. Draw up tables like those above. Observe how different parts of your school's grounds are used at different times and make notes on your table. Write a short report on your findings. Remember to include any areas that are not often used.

2. How do different groups make conflicting demands on the school grounds? For example, do the needs of two different groups clash?

3. Are any groups not catered for very well?

Establishing the needs of your school and the community in relation to the school grounds

Before any ideas for improvement can be suggested, you must complete a survey of the school grounds. Draw a map showing features like trees, benches, footpaths, sports pitches and courts. On the right is such a map for a typical school.

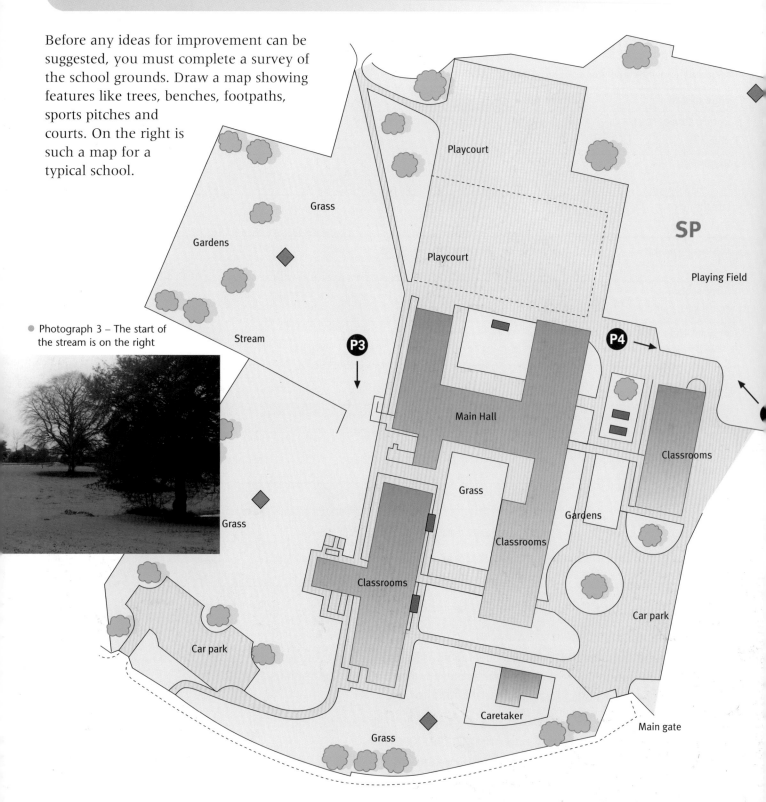

● Photograph 3 – The start of the stream is on the right

Gardens

Grass

Stream

SP

Playing Field

Playcourt

Playcourt

P3

P4

Main Hall

Classrooms

Grass

Classrooms

Gardens

Grass

Classrooms

Car park

Car park

Caretaker

Grass

Main gate

● Photograph 4 – Looking from the car park towards the floodlit all-weather pitch

SP

All-weather pitch

P2

	Trees
	Benches
	Footpaths
SP	Sports pitches
P2	Location of photographs
	Under-used areas

● Photograph 1 – Looking across a typical school playing field

● Photograph 2 – Looking towards the playcourts

How can you decide how to develop the school grounds?

Many groups use school grounds, including people of different ages, sexes and cultural backgrounds, as well as people with more or less mobility. Therefore, you might need to prioritise your plans.

There are many possibilities for developing school grounds. Here are just a few of the things you could include:

- an environmental area
- different sporting facilities
- a quiet area for thought and reflection
- an art and crafts area
- a temporary caravan site during the holidays
- a cultural and entertainment area
- a nature or garden area
- a waste recycling area
- a small-scale farming area.

Some of these ideas can be seen in the photographs.

● A cultural and entertainment area

● A small farm in school grounds

Activities

1 Who would benefit from each of these possible developments? Discuss this in small groups and report back to the class.

2 How would these developments help to improve the quality of life for:
- you personally
- the school as a whole
- the wider community?

3 Can you see any problems with some of these developments?

4 How could you make decisions about what should be included in the development of the school grounds?

5 Who should be involved in managing any developments?

How can you meet the needs of people who use the school grounds?

It is important that opportunities are provided for differing cultures and ethnic identities. Here are a few ideas:

- designing and creating a mural
- re-creating an environment from another country
- creating a spiritual or peace garden.

It is also important that these projects are sustainable. Some could involve relevant local and national voluntary and community groups, who could advise, assist with and benefit from their development. Such organisations could include:

- a local wildlife group
- the Arts Council
- the local council
- church and other religious groups
- foreign embassies
- groups representing the disabled
- local companies
- national charities.

It is also very important to take into account other people's views so consult – or talk to – everyone involved with your plan.

Getting technical

Sustainable development meeting the needs of the present without affecting the ability of future generations to meet their own needs.

Consultation talking to other people who have an interest in a project.

Ethnic identity the cultural group to which a person belongs.

Activities

1. What improvements might help provide for the needs of users already identified, such as the disabled or the elderly?

2. Who will need to be involved in order to maintain such projects?

3. Who could be involved in the future?

4. On a plan of your school grounds, decide where a variety of activities could take place. Remember to consider as many groups of people as possible.

5. How could local voluntary and community groups link into your plans?

6. Use a range of sources to look for other solutions to the needs of various users of school grounds. Look at magazines, newspapers, videos, leaflets from local and national organisations and websites of suppliers of equipment.

Planning and making changes to your school grounds

We have seen some ideas on possible improvements to school grounds. It is now time to consider how you can participate in changing the management and appearance of your own school grounds. You may feel strongly about how the grounds are used during breaks and lunchtimes, or have some ideas on how best to use an area that you feel is not used to its full potential.

Before any changes can take place, a lot of planning will be involved. The diagram on the right takes you through some of the stages of development.

Stage 1
Decide on a project after widespread consultation

Stage 2
Cost different aspects and draw up a budget

Stage 3
Find out about funding, e.g. council grants or charities

Stage 4
Decide on a project after widespread consultation

Stage 5
Find out the best place to deposit the money raised to get the best rate of interest

Stage 6
Organise people and times to carry out the project

Stage 7
Organise an opening ceremony and invite all those who have been involved

Stage 8
Reflect on individual and group contributions, consider what went well and what could have been better

Stage 9
Think about how the impact of the project could be monitered so as to make future projects more effective

Activities

1. Look carefully at the diagram on the right. What difficulties could arise during the various stages?

2. What fund-raising events can you think of?

3. Why is it necessary to look back and think about the project once it is completed?

4. If you had to make a short speech at the opening ceremony, what three main points would you make?

An example of a school grounds project: The green area, Crispin School, Somerset

As part of an environmental awareness campaign, pupils and staff of Crispin School in Street, Somerset, have converted an area in their school grounds from old gardens and waste ground into a 'green area' containing a small nature reserve and classroom.

Some of the features of the project are:

- the nature reserve is also used as an area for quiet reflection
- the classroom is made entirely from recycled materials
- the classroom is powered by its own small wind turbine
- the nature reserve contains examples of old rural crafts such as wicker work
- the classroom is used by outside organisations such the Worldwide Fund for Nature and Sustainable Somerset and local primary schools
- it was funded by a combination of grants from various local and national organisations and school funds
- it is used by many different subjects in the school, including Science, Technology, RE and Geography
- it is maintained and monitored by both staff and pupils.

The idea came originally from the school staff, but there has been involvement by local voluntary organisations, national charities, Somerset County Council, local companies and school pupils.

Activities

1. Think of an area of your school grounds where a project of this type could be undertaken. What would be the advantages of such a project in your school?

2. What might be some of the problems in setting up such a project?

3. What would you find most appealing about this area?

● The green area classroom

● Inside the nature reserve

Case Study 1: New Eccles Hall School, Norwich

Nearly all of the pupils at New Eccles Hall School in Eccles, Norfolk helped to design and create an outdoor mosaic tile seating area, within the school grounds, under the guidance of artist in residence Vic Ellis. The seating, which includes coloured tiles forming the mosaic, has been personalised with the names of all pupils and members of staff involved written into the clay.

The children were asked to design the seating area and decide where it should be situated within the school. Ms Ellis wanted the seating area to represent the ideas of the children, while at the same time involve her own work. Many different designs were produced and, although good, many had to be rejected due to impracticality and cost. The designs ranged from glass-walled seating to fountains but, with the advice of Ms Ellis, a combination of ideas were chosen and integrated into the final mosaic design.

With the final design complete, work began on transforming the ideas into reality with children in years 7 and 8 getting involved in the production of the tiles. As the location of the project was in a grass area, cement foundations had to be laid with the help of local construction workers. The creation of the seating itself involved rolling the individual detailed designs into the clay tiles, which the pupils carried out using their own designs. Additional tiles then formed the school crest in the centre with bench seats around the outside containing the name-inscriptions in the clay. The project used around £40 worth of clay and £200 was spent on firing the tiles and blocks, which was financed by the school.

The school are extremely pleased with what has been produced and head teacher Richard Allard commented that Vic Ellis has inspired pupils. 'The pupils have seen a professional artist at work and have been able to try their own hand at it. The seat is a great tribute to her work and will be a lasting memory'. The project has been a great success and has helped pupils to contribute something to their school while integrating different years and departments.

Activities

1. What did the pupils do in their project?
2. Give one result of the project

Case study 2: Royton and Crompton School, Oldham, Lancashire

Pupils at Royton and Crompton School in Oldham have been heavily involved in the development and management of their school grounds as part of the 'Education for sustainable development' scheme. Approximately 1,200 pupils in Key Stages 3 and 4, led by a team of teachers, formed an 'Environment group' along with governors and other school staff. The project was designed to improve the environment of the school. It was funded by money raised by landfill tax and managed by Groundwork, a federation of Trusts in England, Wales and Northern Ireland aiming to improve the quality of local environments.

The project for improving part of the school site took several years to complete. Initially, pupils worked with the local authority, environmental groups and a number of other organisations to develop a plan. After this, the project was mainly conducted by the pupils. The area the group decided to develop was not being used at the time, other than for dumping rubbish and exercising dogs.

One of the project's main aims was to protect and enhance the school environment by developing a nature and activity area. It was felt that this would benefit both the school and the wider community. Pupils could be involved in planning and managing the project, while at the same time improving the opportunities that the school offered for physical and social recreation.

The first stage of the project was to carry out an ecological survey of the site. A group of pupils volunteered to carry out this research alongside Groundwork. They used the results from the survey to plan suitable developments for different parts of the site. As a result of discussion groups with landscape architects, the pupils agreed to divide the site into different areas. They planned a woodland plantation, a wetland area, a wildflower area, a quiet area at the centre and a trail around the edge. They worked with a local environmental group to collect saplings from a local nature reserve. They also raised money to purchase wildflowers and planted trees which were donated by local organisations.

Although many local organisations were involved, it was the pupils who designed and managed the project. They organised fund-raising events and used Computer Aided Design (CAD) program to accurately map the area and its contents. The pupils also made allowances for the needs of everyone in the community, with particular attention to detail. For example, the trail surrounding and within the area was designed for wheelchair access, in terms of its width and the materials used. More recently, artists in residence have worked with pupils to create sculptures throughout the school grounds, and work continues to go into the development and maintenance of the area.

Both pupils and staff have learned a tremendous amount from this successful project. It has taught pupils about identifying a problem and working together in order to find a solution that benefits everyone. By bringing them into contact with the local community, the project has developed their sense of responsibility and citizenship. This has led to further projects with different departments working together to improve the facilities of the school. For example, GCSE PE pupils are developing more 'physical activity' areas and Design and Technology pupils have created a pond area with benches and wildlife.

Activities

1. What were the aims of the project?
2. Who was involved in it?
3. What has it taught the pupils?

Case study 3: Dorton House School, Seal, Kent

Work has begun at Dorton House School in Seal, Kent, to transform a currently underused area of the grounds into a 'real-life learning zone', focusing on aquatic life and horticulture. The school, which is for visually impaired children aged 5–16, was selected as a 2001 Barclays New Futures Award Winner and was awarded £3000 to offer its students more opportunities to develop skills for life, work and citizenship.

The project is led by Anna Stevenson, Life Skills Programme Co-ordinator at Dorton House. It aims to develop an area within the school into something that will combine art, maths, ICT, science and life skills. All pupils in the school are involved with the project, but Year 10 pupils are involved in the design, project management, budgeting and maintenance of the area. The pupils at Dorton House will also be working with sighted pupils from other local schools and other organisations, in order to raise awareness of visual impairment.

Although the school received prize money from Barclays bank, the staff and pupils felt that they also wanted to contribute by setting up fund-raising events. The pupils began by selling cakes and biscuits at their school. The school radio station, run by pupils, broadcast a sponsored 24-hour radio programme, and other sponsored events, such as silences, were organised. Overall, the pupils raised around £700 to contribute to the project. In order to raise awareness of the project and the school, a 'Groundforce' day was organised, where members of the local community helped clear the area ready for work to begin.

Pupils designed and distributed questionnaires throughout the school and used the results to aid their designs. Using the information they collected, the pupils began to create their ideas for the project and put their designs to Ms Stevenson. It was important that the area to be developed should be educational, in order to enable the pupils to work and learn through experimental activities in a safe environment. Because of this, the ideas were for an area that was functional, quiet and accessible to all pupils, e.g. correct path width and gradient for wheelchair access.

The project has helped to bring the school closer to other schools and organisations in the area, and has raised awareness of visual impairment. The pupils have worked hard and the project looks likely to succeed in creating a relaxing, educational area for the whole school to enjoy and use. The learning zone will be an addition to the other projects that have been carried out at Dorton House such as the Willow Tree Sculptures, which the children worked on with a local artist.

Activities

1. What was the project at Dorton House School?

2. How was the 'real-life learning zone' project funded?

3. What have been the results of the project?

Case study 4: Ivybridge Community College, Devon

Pupils attending Ivybridge Community College in Devon have taken on the problem of waste disposal and recycling within their school grounds, amongst other environmental issues. A group of Year 8 pupils, supported by Citizenship co-ordinator Karl Sweeney, have formed an environmental group known as the 'Green-team'.

This group began a physical survey of the school grounds. They identified, analysed and photographed the areas they felt were the worst in terms of neglect, litter and other forms of rubbish. They then put together a report detailing what they had found and presented it to their year council with proposals outlining their ideas for action. The pupils next contacted their District Council for advice and received permission for an allocation of extra boxes for recycled paper for the areas described in the report. Once the units had been received, the team got together and installed them around the school.

When the units had been installed and the school's pupils and staff knew where they were located, the team began weekly maintenance work on the areas, e.g. emptying units, clearing litter. However, since the team did not feel this was satisfactory, they drew up another proposal for the District Council and the Local Education Authority (LEA) requesting a larger recycling unit to be installed within the school grounds. Both agreed to fund the project and the unit has since been installed. Proposals for two more units for recycling aluminium and glass have now been drawn up and the local authorities have again approved the plans.

Since the project began, more and more pupils at the school have wanted to get involved and more proposals for developments have been produced. Year 10 pupils have approached the senior management of the school, asking for bike sheds to be introduced in a bid to reduce traffic in the area. Other proposals include the installation of more drinking fountains and healthy food machines in the school. What began as a small group of Year 8 pupils with an interest in the environment has become a surge of interest in the improvement of the school and community surroundings, with all year groups interested and junior sports leaders working with local primary schools and other areas of the community.

Activities

1. How did the pupils plan where to develop?

2. What were the problems that the group aimed to solve?

3. Who was involved in the project?

Index